You've Got to Be Believed
to Be Heard

You've Got to Be

Believed

to Be Heard

Revised and Updated Edition

Bert Decker

ST. MARTIN'S PRESS ≋ NEW YORK

YOU'VE GOT TO BE BELIEVED TO BE HEARD. Copyright © 2008 by Bert Decker. All rights reserved. Printed in the United States of America. For information, address St. Martin's Press, 175 Fifth Avenue, New York, N.Y. 10010.

www.stmartins.com

Library of Congress Cataloging-in-Publication Data

Decker, Bert.
    You've got to be believed to be heard : the complete book of speaking—in business and in life! / Bert Decker.
        p. cm.
    ISBN-13: 978-0-312-37469-3
    ISBN-10: 0-312-37469-0
  1. Oral communication.   2. Business communication.   I. Title.
    P95.D42 2008
    302.2'242—dc22

                                                                2007032560

First Edition: September 2008

10 9 8 7 6 5 4 3 2 1

Contents

Part V: From Information to Influence

Preface

When the first edition of this book came out, little did I know that it would become a speaking classic.

I have written several books since, but none that have stayed in such continuous demand as this. So it is a thrill not only to revise and update the stories and concepts concerning the *behavior* of communications, but to add an entirely new section on the *content* of communications.

Here for the first time you have the "Complete Book of Speaking," which contains all you need to become a great communicator in both form and function, behavior and content. With the publication here of the Decker Grid System you will *always* be able to create a focused and listener-based message—no matter what the circumstances or setting. If you often speak in a business environment, you will avoid the plague of data dumps and PowerPoint abuse. And if you want your personal, professional, and relational communications to be more focused and effective, the Grid will do that for you too. You can truly create your own communication experience in all your circumstances.

In the first edition, I gave many thanks to many people, as that was my first major book. And I do not diminish by one iota the indebtedness I feel to the influence of my family, associates, and the dozens of co-laborers at Decker Communications over the last quarter century, or for the contribution of Jim Denney, a topflight professional writer, who also collaborated with me on the first edition.

For this edition I want to single out my wife and two other unique people who are my partners in Decker Communications, Inc. First, my wife, Dru Scott Decker, who is also a well-known author and speaker, was an immeasurable help—not just for ideas and feedback, but in the continuous discussions we have on communication and concepts that stimulate and influence my thinking. That adds up to a lot of insight and knowledge over these years, and I am thankful.

And as for my son and daughter-in-law, Ben and Kelly Decker, I am grateful for their ideas, competence, spirit, and inspiration as we have relaunched the "new" Decker Communications, Inc. They have provided a fresh perspective and have enabled us to establish a new platform to carry on the legacy of communications excellence to hundreds of thousands of people. And they are fun to work with.

I hope this book will help you create your own distinctive communication experience in your personal and professional life. That is its goal, and if you execute the suggestions within, I believe that you will be more powerful and influential than you thought you ever could be.

—BERT DECKER
San Francisco, 2008

You've Got to Be Believed to Be Heard

Introduction

A Leader Put to the Test

The events of September 11, 2001, could not have been worse. The terrorist attacks were seared in the hearts of Americans because we saw them happen in immediate color.

But the aftermath of fear, terror, and suspicion could have been worse—much worse. And communication made the difference.

It was eight months into the presidency of George W. Bush. Mr. Bush was known primarily as a master of mangled syntax who had eked out a win in the narrowest election in history. He ran neck and neck with opponent Al Gore, a notoriously dull, dry speech-maker. As communicators, Gore was no Bill Clinton and Bush was no Ronald Reagan.

On the evening of the attacks, President Bush spoke to the American people from the White House.

"These acts of mass murder," he said, "were intended to frighten our nation into chaos and retreat. But they have failed. Our country is strong. A great people has been moved to defend a great nation. . . . None of us will ever forget this day, yet we go forward to defend freedom and all that is good and just in our world." As important as the words he spoke was his behavior—eyes steady, jaw resolute, shoulders firm. This was not the campaigner we had seen months before. This was a leader who was authentic. The speeches President Bush delivered that day gave the American people the sense that this man was ready to lead.

Three days later, Friday, September 14, 2001, President Bush went to Washington Cathedral and gave what many consider the most eloquent speech of his presidency. He began in Lincolnesque form with words worthy of the Gettysburg Address. "We are here in the middle hour of our grief," he said. "So many have suffered so great a loss, and today we express our nation's sorrow. We come before God to pray for the missing and the dead, and for those who loved them."

He spoke as the commander in chief, appealing to our resolute strength and unity as Americans. He became America's chaplain, saying, "Grief and tragedy and hatred are only for a time. Goodness, remembrance and love have no end, and the Lord of Life holds all who die and all who mourn."

He inspired us with stories, briefly told, to remind us of the heroes of that day: "Inside the World Trade Center, one man who could have saved himself stayed until the end at the side of his quadriplegic friend. A beloved priest died giving the last rites to a firefighter. Two office workers, finding a disabled stranger, carried her down sixty-eight floors to safety. A group of men drove through the night from Dallas to Washington to bring skin grafts for burned victims."

It was a memorable speech—but even more memorable was the speech he gave just a few hours later. He flew to New York and arrived at the sacred ground where the towers had stood. Now dressed in blue jeans and a brown jacket with an open collar, he was greeted by iron-workers and firemen shouting, "U-S-A! U-S-A!"

The president walked and shook hands and shouted encouragement. Then he jumped up onto a fire truck with the help of retired fireman Bob Beckwith, who was working at ground zero as an unpaid volunteer. Beckwith was about to climb down, but the president said, "Stay right here," and put his arm around the man.

As the chants of "U-S-A!" died down, someone handed a bullhorn to the president. "I want you all to know," Mr. Bush said, "that America today is on bended knee in prayer for the people whose lives were lost here, for the workers who work here, for the families who mourn."

"I can't hear you!" someone in the crowd shouted.

"I can hear you!" the president shouted back through the bullhorn

President George W. Bush (*left*), standing next to retired firefighter Bob Beckwith, speaking at the site of the World Trade Center on September 14, 2001. (PAUL J. RICHARDS/AFP/GETTY IMAGES)

amid applause and cheers. "The rest of the world hears you! And the people who knocked these buildings down will hear all of us soon!"

The applause and shouts of "U-S-A! U-S-A!" grew louder, and the president paused until the chanting subsided. "The nation sends its love and compassion to everybody who is here," he concluded. "Thank you for your hard work. Thank you for making the nation proud. And may God bless America."

Becoming a President for All

What happened? Did the inept communicator get coaching? Did Bush decide to communicate like Clinton? What was the transformation?

President George W. Bush became authentic. He was not trying to play the role of president, as he had appeared to before. He *was* the president. He deeply felt this event and thus he felt his words, and he communicated that feeling. He was real, and authentic, and he had finally reached the First Brain of the American People.

In June 2003, Pulitzer prize–winning journalist Carl Cannon of the nonpartisan weekly *National Journal* reflected on what has come to be known as the "Bullhorn Speech." He said, "If we didn't have confidence in him as a communicator, we didn't have confidence in him to do anything. So when Bush does that [the Bullhorn Speech], he really in that moment becomes a President for all the people, and a person that even people who didn't vote for him . . . can look to as their Commander-in-Chief." [1]

This is a profound insight: When people have confidence in someone as a communicator, they have confidence in that person, period. The ability to communicate is essential to leadership. It's indispensable to persuasion. It's crucial to the ability to motivate, inspire, energize, galvanize, and mobilize an individual or a nation. The ability to communicate is the key to selling, whether you are selling a product, an idea, a political agenda, or a vision for the future.

A Duty to Communicate

Regardless of our political views, we can all relate to Mr. Bush in this sense. Few of us are naturally effective at communicating—and fewer still *enjoy* speaking before audiences. But when our circumstances demand greatness, we can rise to the challenge. We can all learn to be more effective communicators.

Mr. Bush's approval ratings peaked at 90 percent soon after 9/11, and then began a downward spiral. What accounted for this disastrous slide? For one thing, the war in Iraq was itself under continuous attack, being described in the media as a disaster—and Mr. Bush was saying little to counter that portrayal.

Then came Hurricane Katrina. Once more the American people had horrors seared into their hearts as they could see the tragedy unfold on live television—this time a disaster wreaked by nature instead of man. And this time, where was the leadership? After four days, Mr. Bush strode into an aircraft hangar in Mobile, Alabama, to be briefed on the Katrina response. Greeting FEMA director Michael Brown, he said, "Brownie, you're doing a heck of a job!" To millions of viewers, Mr. Bush seemed shockingly out of touch with reality. The situation cried out for another Bullhorn Speech. The president's response seemed more bull than bullhorn.

By April 2006, Mr. Bush's approval ratings hit rock bottom. His presidency appeared to be on life support. Ironically, while his rankings were at an all-time low, the economy was astonishingly strong. The Dow Jones Industrial Average was approaching an all-time high. The nation was ringing up record retail sales. Unemployment was below 5 percent. The gross domestic product had grown 4.8 percent in the previous quarter. Minority-owned businesses were experiencing a dramatic upswing. And yet—

The Simple Secret of Effective Communicating

The message for all of us is clear: Whatever our life goals, our career goals, or our dreams of a better world, the key to success lies in our ability to communicate. No matter how uncomfortable or ill-equipped we feel as communicators, we dare not back away from the challenge of becoming effective speakers.

Short on skills? We can learn them. Short on confidence? We can gain it. Short on experience? We can make our own opportunities.

In this book, you will discover the secret to effective communicating, a secret that many political leaders, business leaders, sales leaders, and others have failed to learn—much to their detriment. It's the simple secret of reaching the "First Brain." Do you want that promotion or better-paying job? Do you want to make that critical sale? Find that richer relationship? Lead your team, your church, your corporation, your nation to some grand visionary goal? Whatever you want to achieve in life can be yours through the power of the First Brain.

This discovery will place enormous power in your hands—the ability to connect with others through believability and trust. The First Brain is our *emotional* brain. It is real. It is physical. And it is powerful. Neglect it, ignore it, fail to harness its power—and you'll miss out on the most transformational tool for reaching other people and achieving your goals. Understand it and use it—and you'll know how to persuade an audience of one or an audience of millions. No longer will you communicate merely to dispense information; you'll make an *emotional connection* with your listeners—a connection that will enable you to achieve your goals.

Not only will you learn to reach the First Brain of your listeners, you'll also learn how to master your own First Brain to overcome the fear of speaking before audiences—an anxiety common to us all. Even though public speaking is my life, I know what the fear of speaking feels like. I've learned how to transform that emotional tension into positive communicating energy—and I'll share those secrets with you in these pages.

I've been immersed in the communication field for decades. My company has trained more than two hundred thousand leaders, managers, salespeople, and professionals. I have personally coached Charles Schwab, House Speaker Nancy Pelosi, and five-time gold medal Olympian Bonnie Blair, as well as many other leaders and influencers. I've appeared on NBC's *Today* show numerous times.

I've made a lifelong study of the psychology of communication and persuasion. I've seen it proven again and again: The effectiveness of our spoken communication determines the effectiveness of our lives—yet our colleges and universities don't teach people how to communicate effectively. Instead, they teach a dry, academic approach to "public speaking" that involves little more than speaking words written on three-by-five-inch index cards. I've written this book to share my discoveries with you and to show you a better way to communicate.

The first edition of this book has been continuously in print since March 1992. This newly revised and expanded edition updates the information in the original book and adds many powerful new communicating tools, including the revolutionary Decker Grid. By reading this book and applying these principles, you'll gain the skill that some of the top political, professional, and business leaders in the nation have paid thousands to obtain.

Don't worry about having to wade through a lot of technical jargon. This is a practical, user-friendly book. You'll be able to put its principles into effect even before you've finished reading. By the time you're done, you'll be thinking "First Brain" in every communicating situation.

So read on—and open a new chapter in your communicating life!

Part I

The Emotional Connection

CHAPTER 1

The New Communicators

Presidential elections are primarily determined by the communications ability of the candidates. Look at John Kennedy upsetting Richard Nixon, Ronald Reagan beating Michael Dukakis, Bill Clinton defeating George H. W. Bush. And even look at George W. Bush versus either Al Gore or John Kerry, where you had the battles of the "noncommunicators," and both elections went down to the wire.

Of course there's more to it than *just* communications. But the importance of reaching the trust level of the voter is paramount in getting buy-in, and that is what this book is about. For even though we aren't running for president, we are running for the votes of people that we want to influence—be they our customers or employees, or friends and family.

People who are successful at influencing are the people I call the New Communicators, and there are certain things they do.

Being Wrong Proved Me Right

I made a bold prediction in the first edition of this book. I talked about how Dan Rather had doomed the *CBS Evening News* to the ratings cellar because of his dismal "First-Brain-unfriendly" communicating skills. I wrote, "If Rather isn't out of his anchorman job by the time you read this, he probably will be soon."

Well, I was wrong. Those words were published in 1992, and Dan

Rather didn't get the boot from CBS until March 2005, thirteen years after I made that prediction. So I admit it, I was wrong—not about Dan Rather, but about CBS. I never imagined that the suits and bean counters at the Columbia Broadcasting System would willingly forego revenue and stubbornly back a proven money-loser in the anchor chair. But that's exactly what they did.

When CBS finally eased Dan Rather out of the anchor's chair, the tipping point was a scandal involving a *60 Minutes* story he reported and backed up with forged documents. But as Ken Auletta, columnist for *The New Yorker,* pointed out on the PBS *NewsHour with Jim Lehrer* (June 20, 2006), Rather's dismissal was already in the works "because for ten years Dan Rather was in third place and stalled there and didn't seem like he was moving in the evening news race."

What was it about Dan Rather that consistently made him the third man in a three-man race? When he succeeded Walter Cronkite, Rather certainly had the experience, visibility, and credentials to deliver the news. In highly charged confrontations with presidents, and in the combative *60 Minutes* arena, Rather had proved he could make the airwaves crackle with electricity. But the moment he ascended to the anchor chair, viewers defected to NBC and ABC. Ratings for the *CBS Evening News* plummeted.

The CBS brass panicked. Something was wrong with their star newsman, and they didn't know how to fix it. They tried softening his image by dressing him in fuzzy sweaters. They added snazzy computer graphics and built a new set around him. They took away his desk and had him read the news standing up. Later, they tried pairing Rather with newswoman Connie Chung—another disastrous experiment. In short, they changed everything but what really needed to be changed: Dan Rather himself.

As I wrote in this book's first edition, "The upper echelons at CBS still don't seem to grasp what it is that enhances or diminishes trust in their on-screen talent. That's why CBS continues to run a third-rated (and, in terms of effective communication, third-rate) news operation." As history has shown, CBS continued its third-rate performance for thirteen years after I made that statement.

Dan Rather (FREDERICK M. BROWN/GETTY IMAGES)

What was wrong with Dan Rather? Why didn't he attract a bigger audience? To put it simply, Rather is an Old Communicator. He doesn't understand how to make an emotional connection with his viewers. He appears affected, distant, and aloof. His upper lip stiffens when he talks, giving the impression that he's holding something back. These are not details a viewer would consciously notice. But the most important dimension of communication takes place not at the conscious level, but the unconscious level. We're talking about trust, believability, and likability—the emotional connection.

Time magazine offered this appraisal of Dan Rather: "Combative and high-strung, Dan Rather remains more reporter than anchorman. . . . Rather has never seemed completely comfortable in the anchor chair. A courtly and painstakingly polite man in person, he seems stiff and tense on camera. Even his attempts at spontaneity and good humor look programmed."[1]

An anchorman who seems "uncomfortable," "combative," and "high-strung" is not likely to win ratings points for his network. Ratings points equal dollars—millions and millions of advertising dollars. CBS may have proved me wrong in my 1992 prediction about Dan Rather's future—but it cost CBS millions to do so. And what did those millions of dollars of lost advertising revenue prove?

Why, they proved me right, of course!

Old Communicators and New Communicators

New Communicators are those who will take charge, but will mobilize resources. They tap into their natural energy, but don't overdo it. They are prepared, but don't read speeches. The New Communicators are those who are successful in their communications and connections, where the Old Communicators are not.

A classic case is that of the late Hall of Fame football coach Bill Walsh. Walsh served as head coach of the San Francisco 49ers for ten years. During that time, he perfected a unique offensive playbook called the West Coast Offense and led his team to Super Bowl championships in 1981, 1984, and 1988. He was inducted into the Pro Football Hall of Fame in 1993. A technically precise, flawlessly gifted leader, Walsh was also ruggedly handsome and photogenic. When he announced that he had leukemia he had an outpouring of sympathy from fans. He was popular, but he was no New Communicator.

Following his retirement from coaching in 1988, Walsh seemed destined for a successful career as a TV sportscaster. He went to work for NBC and had everything going for him: a brilliant mind, knowledge of the game, good looks, and phenomenal past success. Yet three years later, his broadcast career was over. What happened?

The problem was simply this: Bill Walsh didn't connect with viewers. He rarely smiled. He showed little emotion, passion, or animation when he spoke. His fame and success on the field should have garnered him a long career as a broadcaster and advertising endorser. Instead, he washed out.

Compare Bill Walsh with John Madden. Now there's a coach who has cashed in on his gridiron glory! After ten years as head coach of the Oakland Raiders (1969 to 1978 with a Super Bowl championship in 1977), Madden has enjoyed a broadcast career lasting more than a quarter of a century. He's been a football commentator for CBS, Fox, ABC, and NBC and has received fourteen Emmys for Outstanding Sports Personality, plus the Golden Mike Award.

The list of products and companies John Madden has endorsed includes Miller Lite beer, Ace Hardware, Toyota, Outback Steakhouse, Verizon Wireless, Rent-A-Center, and Sirius Satellite Radio. He played himself in the movie *Little Giants* and hosted a segment of NBC's *Saturday Night Live*. His voice lends authenticity to the *Madden NFL* football-simulation software produced by EA Sports—a perennial best-seller among video games.

According to RaidersOnline.org, Madden's earnings from all sources top forty million dollars a year. Not bad wages for a guy with a face that would make a freight train take a dirt road! Madden didn't plan a career as a communicator and product pitchman. When he

John Madden (SCOTT BOEHM/GETTY IMAGES)

retired from football, he figured he'd go into real estate with a friend. His first day on the job, he spent a few hours in line at the town hall in Pleasanton, California, waiting to get a sewer permit for a shopping mall. His first day in real estate was also his last.

Today, John Madden is a superstar—not because of his coaching ability, but because he is a New Communicator. Above all, he's energetic, and also honest, natural, likable, and believable. That's the big difference between John Madden and Bill Walsh—and the difference between their respective paychecks: John Madden reaches our First Brain. Bill Walsh did not.

An Old Communicator uses the spoken word to dispense information. A New Communicator uses not only the spoken word, but personal energy, enthusiasm, eye communication, gestures, and more to make an emotional connection with the listener.

Old Communicators fail. New Communicators succeed.

Some of the Best . . . and Worst

Let's contrast some New Communicators with some Old Communicators—and I think you'll see exactly what I mean.

THE NEW

STEVE JOBS is a uniquely effective presenter for Apple Computers. He has mythic status as the guy who started a global computer empire in his parents' garage. Over the years, Apple has repeatedly been declared dead by the pundits, and each time Steve Jobs has engineered a resurrection. Jobs has been an effective business leader because he is always focused on the user experience, not gadgetry. And he's effective as a speaker because he's focused on the audience experience, not on dispensing data.

His approach to communication is disarmingly simple. When he takes the stage, he looks like a guy in jeans and a black shirt talking off the cuff. He eschews lectern and notes. Steve won't allow anything to come between himself and his audience. He demonstrates the product he's unveiling with a sense of humor, excitement, and enthusiasm—and an element of surprise. His tone is genial, relaxed, and friendly, never hard sell. He uses black slides (see page 235) and mostly pictures in his PowerPoints.

When Steve Jobs speaks at the Macworld conference and Expo every January, he is treated like a rock star. His little expo is about one-tenth the size of the massive Comdex tech show in Las Vegas a couple of weeks later. Yet because of his impact and influence, Macworld and Jobs get more publicity than Comdex.

THE OLD

LEE RAYMOND, the former CEO of Exxon Mobil, is symbolic of the worst instincts of major corporations when they find themselves facing a PR problem. After Hurricanes Katrina and Wilma in late 2005, the price of gasoline rose sharply across the United States. Oil companies were accused of price-gouging. Exxon Mobil, which posted record single-quarter profits of $9.9 billion, was widely regarded as the worst offender.

Steve Jobs (JUSTIN SULLIVAN/GETTY IMAGES)

Lee Raymond (CHIP SOMODEVILLA/GETTY IMAGES)

On November 9, 2005, Raymond appeared at a Senate hearing to justify Exxon Mobil's prices and lavish profits. Raymond was a classic Old Communicator—gruff, combative, and defensive. His speaking style was unanimated and obfuscatory. He radiated arrogance and an attitude that he didn't owe anyone an explanation. His performance was viewed by media pundits as stonewalling.

Less than two months later, Raymond retired and set off another media uproar when it was revealed that his retirement package was valued at nearly four hundred million dollars—then the largest in U.S. corporate history. No question, Lee Raymond is a very wealthy man, but he is also one of the most distrusted and disliked people in American business. Even after his retirement, his unlikable persona symbolizes the public perception of Exxon Mobil.

THE NEW

OPRAH WINFREY has been talking on TV since she was nineteen, and she has never been better. Open, vulnerable, funny, and compassionate, Oprah has become a conglomerate through her communication

Oprah Winfrey (EVAN AGOSTINI/GETTY IMAGES)

ability. She has a special gift of empathy with her audience. She not only talks, but she receives a vibe from the audience that keeps her continuously connected. The ability to receive that vibe is a learnable skill.

Oprah's first TV job paid ten thousand dollars a year. Her financial ambition was, as she put it, "to make my age"—and at age twenty-two she was indeed making twenty-two thousand. She could hardly imagine being forty and making forty thousand; she certain didn't dare to dream of being a billionaire at age forty!

Her life has been transformed by her ability to communicate—and she encourages others to follow her example. In the March 2003 issue of *O, The Oprah Magazine,* she offered some sound advice on communicating before an audience: "A powerful beginning and ending will stick with your listeners. What's the most important message you want to leave your audience with—and why should they care? Every listener instinctively wants to know one thing. What's in it for me? The greatest public speakers are those who work at making their addresses both interesting and relatable."[2]

Oprah connects with emotion and storytelling. She communicates with enthusiasm and vulnerability. When she interviews a heroic single mother or a child bravely confronting a fatal illness or a 9/11 widow, her eyes tear up and she keeps speaking with a catch in her throat. She's real—and audiences know it. She may be a billionaire, but deep down, she's one of them. She has talked her way into America's heart, and the connection people feel with her is the foundation of her amazing success.

THE OLD

JEANINE PIRRO is an attractive New York State politician who announced her candidacy for the United States Senate on August 10, 2005. Her goal was to unseat incumbent senator Hillary Rodham Clinton. Clearly, Pirro had made up her mind to bat in the big leagues. But when she stepped up to the plate, she didn't even look ready for the little leagues.

She immediately got off on the wrong foot by standing at a lectern to read a prepared statement. Reading is boring. Worse, reading a speech makes the speaker look inauthentic and unenthusiastic. But for

Jeanine Pirro (PAUL HAWTHORNE/GETTY IMAGES)

Ms. Pirro, reading led to a communications catastrophe. In the middle of her speech, she stopped in midsentence. As the audience waited and the cameras rolled, she fumbled with papers for a full thirty-two seconds of awkward silence. Finally, she turned to her staff and asked, "Does anyone have page ten?"

It was a faux pas of the first magnitude—and her lackluster speaking skills continued to drag her down for the next few months of the campaign. As her fund-raising efforts foundered and polling showed her trailing Mrs. Clinton 62 percent to 30 percent, the ruling powers of the party leaned on her to quit the race. Four days before Christmas 2005, she yielded to the inevitable and threw in the towel.

Of course, losing didn't have to be inevitable. If Jeanine Pirro had invested some time in acquiring more effective communicating skills, she wouldn't have lost page ten—and she would have had a fighting chance at the polls.

THE NEW

HOWARD SCHULTZ grew up poor in the federally subsidized Bayview housing project in Brooklyn, New York. Today he is head of the Seattle-based Starbucks coffee empire. He reached the top in large part on the strength of his communication skills.

Though often called the "founder" of Starbucks, Schultz actually joined the company in 1982. At that time, Starbucks didn't sell brewed coffee, only roasted beans. Schultz left Starbucks in 1985, formed his own company, Il Giornale, and later purchased Starbucks and aggressively expanded it into a chain of coffee shops. By the end of 2006, there were more than twelve thousand Starbucks outlets around the world.

Howard Schultz has had three primary audiences to connect with in order to generate his success: investors, employees, and customers. He has used the same set of communications skills to reach all three audiences. Those skills include enthusiasm, storytelling, and emotional connection.

It wasn't always easy for Schultz to convince investors to support his dream of a chain of shops that dispensed not only coffee but a sense of

Howard Schultz (BILL PUGLIANO/GETTY IMAGES)

community. The investors who bought into the Starbucks vision when the company went public in 1992 have received more than a hundred-to-one return. Schultz has successfully sold that same vision to Starbucks consumers, and the result is that many customers now see Starbucks as their home away from home, their retreat away from work.

Starbucks customers are often surprised to look up from their four-dollar venti mocha lattes and see Howard Schultz himself at their table, thanking them for their patronage. He visits at least twenty-five outlets a week to talk to employees and customers, asking questions, picking up suggestions, and communicating with the people who have made him successful.

Schultz also uses his communicating skills to build the sense of camaraderie and teamwork so crucial to the company's ongoing success. He calls Starbucks employees "partners," and new hires undergo several days of acculturation that go far beyond mere training. Schultz wants his partners to exemplify the Starbucks culture—and he wants them to know they are valued. Every Starbucks employee hears directly from Schultz (via video presentation) that he's happy to have them on his team. As a result, the Starbucks organization has become known worldwide for its high morale and positive corporate culture—an environment Schultz himself has created.

Howard Schultz reflected in an interview in *Business Week*, "Whether I'm talking to a barista, a customer, or investor, I really communicate how I feel about our company, our mission, and our values. It's our collective passion that provides a competitive advantage in the marketplace because we love what we do and we're inspired to do it better."[3]

THE OLD

MICHAEL CHERTOFF, secretary of Homeland Security in the Bush administration, has a lot of responsibilities—and one of them is communicating with the American people, whom he is sworn to protect. The problem is, he doesn't seem to know that. He doesn't communicate to inspire confidence. His demeanor has been described in the media as "abrasive," "chilly," and "intimidating." His speaking style is

Michael Chertoff (KAREN BLEIER/AFP/GETTY IMAGES)

matter-of-fact, rapid-fire, and coldly analytical. The result is an impression of an administrator who is uncaring and even arrogant.

What's worse, Chertoff did not come front and center in the Katrina natural disaster that went on to become a communications disaster. His subordinate, Michael Brown, head of FEMA, was also of the old communications school—with low energy, darting eyes, and a bland voice. Chertoff could have been a leader and taken charge in communicating daily about Katrina, but he chose to stay in the background—letting Brown take the heat. Brown did not inspire confidence, and when Chertoff did step in, the confidence level did not step up. His communications manner was aloof and distancing.

In a profile of Michael Chertoff on National Public Radio, reporter Madeleine Brand observed that the secretary of Homeland security possessed "a prosecutorial demeanor that may not comfort a nation in a time of fear."[4] Indeed. The nation—and the Bush administration—needed someone in that office who inspired trust and confidence, not anxiety.

THE NEW

PAUL HEWSON is the only person ever to have received nominations for an Oscar, a Grammy, a Golden Globe, and a Nobel Peace Prize. You say you've never heard of Paul Hewson? Well, perhaps you know him better as—

BONO, the lead singer of U2.

Born in Dublin in 1960 to a Protestant mother and a Catholic father, Bono has seen his share of economic discrimination and terrorism. He remembers the bombings and random murders of "the Troubles" in Northern Ireland. With his mixed Protestant-Catholic parentage, he always felt he was walking a fence. In 1982, soon after U2 was formed, Bono married his longtime girlfriend, Ali Stewart; today they have four children.

At U2 concerts, Bono does more than rock. He talks. He reaches out to politically disengaged youths and urges them to make their world a better place. He shouts to the crowd, "Our generation is the first that can look poverty and disease in the eye and say, 'We don't have to

Bono (PAUL MCCONNELL/GETTY IMAGES)

stand for this!' We have the resources to make poverty and AIDS a thing of the past." He uses his rock tours to recruit young people to his ONE Campaign against Third World poverty and disease. To date, he's signed up more than a million young people for the cause; his goal is to enlist ten million young activists by 2008.

Bono is a passionate, persuasive New Communicator. His mission in life is to meet with political leaders, religious leaders, financiers, entertainers, journalists, and ordinary people who can lend a hand in solving the problems of poverty and disease in the Third World. He has been interviewed by Oprah, Larry King, and Bill O'Reilly. He's reached out to Warren Buffett, the second richest man in America. He has formed alliances with the unlikeliest of people, including retired conservative senator Jesse Helms of North Carolina, media mogul Rupert Murdoch, and televangelist Pat Robertson. In addition to President Bush, Bono has met with such world leaders as Tony Blair, Jacques Chirac, and Gerhard Schröder—and has convinced them to make financial commitments totaling more than fifty billion dollars a year for Africa's eighteen poorest nations. He's had an audience with Pope John Paul II and taken part in a three-day church conference at Willow Creek Community Church in Illinois, beamed by satellite to seventy thousand pastors around the world.

Bono is smart and articulate, and he tends to pile phrase upon phrase into run-on sentences as his nimble tongue races to keep up with his agile mind. He does his homework and scrupulously checks his facts. He consults with experts and researchers. Then he goes out and confidently recites names, numbers, places, and problems with pinpoint accuracy. There's none of this "close enough for rock and roll" attitude with Bono. If he says it, you can take it to Barclays.

Like all New Communicators, Bono is a storyteller. For example, he tells about the time he and Ali went to Ethiopia to witness the suffering in that country. During Bono's six-week stint as a volunteer in an orphanage, an Ethiopian father brought a small child to him. In broken English, the man pleaded, "You take child. Your child now. Won't die." Bono tearfully had to tell this father no, he couldn't take the child—

and he vowed that it would be the last time he would ever say no to human need.

Another thing Bono does that makes him an effective communicator is to issue a call to action. Sometimes his audience is a crowd of U2 fans. Sometimes it's a staid group of politicians and financiers in Italian suits. It doesn't matter whom he's addressing, he always tells them that God is watching, history is watching, and they must meet the challenge of the moment. He often finds innovative ways to issue the call.

"I used to be a pest, a stone in the shoe," he says. "It was hipper for me to be on the barricades—it looked better on the résumé of a rock-and-roll star. But I've learned that I can do better by going to the White House and talking. If my opinion is informed, then I have the right to express it and not to be afraid of who else is in the room."

Bono is a persuader, a bridge-builder, a forger of unlikely alliances. He's a New Communicator who reaches the First Brain to make the world a better place.

THE OLD

MARK McGWIRE was one of the most powerful hitters ever to play pro baseball, earning such nicknames as "Big Mac" and "Big Red." Over his career, the rusty-haired slugger averaged one home run for every 10.61 times at the plate—the best home-run ratio in the history of the game.

But in an appearance before the House Government Reform Committee on March 17, 2005, Mark McGwire repeatedly struck out. Asked if he used illegal performance-enhancing drugs such as steroids, McGwire stiffly (and repetitiously) replied, "I'm not here to talk about the past." After offering the same numbing answer several times, McGwire tried a different tack: "My lawyers have advised me that I cannot answer these questions without jeopardizing my friends, my family, and myself." When a congressman asked if he was invoking the Fifth Amendment, McGwire went back to his earlier nonresponsive response: "I'm not here to talk about the past. I'm here to be positive about this subject."

When he spoke, McGwire looked anxious and defensive. His eyes flitted and his unsteady voice betrayed emotional strain and a lack of

Mark McGwire testifies before House Committee on Government Reform (MARK WILSON/GETTY IMAGES)

confidence. His words, demeanor, and voice made it clear that he had something to hide. For many fans, his disastrous performance before the House committee has forever overshadowed his stellar performance at the plate.

Mark McGwire went from hero to has-been in one very public poor-communication moment. The public perception of him changed dramatically because he went to the Old Communicator school. Too bad.

A Workable Strategy for Success

The world belongs to the New Communicators. The Old Communicators have missed the opportunity to multiply their success. Why? Because they failed to grasp the secret of the New Communicators—a transformational secret so simple that anyone can take advantage of it.

You may say, "But I'm not a politician or a CEO or an actor or a baseball star! I'm not in the public eye." The truth is, unless you are a cave dweller, you *are* in the public eye. We are *all* in the public eye—and we all have a lot riding on our ability to communicate: A promotion. A big sale. A leadership position. A marriage relationship. A parent-child relationship.

Communicating is a contact sport. Your ability to communicate is the single most important skill determining your success in every aspect of your life. You dare not make the mistake of thinking that communication is nothing but dumping information on another person.

Make that emotional connection with your listeners. Reach their hearts as well as their minds. Reach the First Brain, the emotional brain, to create likability, believability, and trust. Once you acquire the easily learned skills of the New Communicators, you'll find yourself at the top of your profession, gaining the recognition and success you seek.

Because you've read this far, you already know more about effective communicating than some of the brightest minds in business, sports, and politics. You know that effective communication is more than just saying words. Now, keep reading and start building the skills that will enable you to make that emotional connection with your listeners.

The Larrikinesque Noah

When forty-four-year-old Steve Irwin, "The Crocodile Hunter," was killed by a stingray while filming underwater off Australia's Great Barrier Reef in 2006, many news outlets initially reported it as a back-of-the-book story to be quickly forgotten. It soon became apparent, however, that Steve Irwin's death was deeply felt by millions around the world, both young and old. This was a Big Story.

Why did so many people care so deeply about one Australian TV personality? What made him so beloved? Who was the Crocodile Hunter?

Steve Irwin was raised in Queensland, the son of parents who owned the Australia Zoo in

Steve Irwin (JUSTIN SULLIVAN/GETTY IMAGES)

Beerwah. For his sixth birthday, Steve received a twelve-foot python. At age nine, he was wrestling crocodiles under his dad's watchful eye. As a teenager, he was a crocodile trapper, rescuing crocs from populated areas where they might hurt someone or be hurt.

In 1992 he married Terri Raines in Eugene, Oregon. The film of their croc-hunting honeymoon adventure became the pilot episode for a nature show, *The Crocodile Hunter*. After debuting in Australia in 1996, the show moved to American TV in 1997. *The Crocodile Hunter* was a hit, and was soon reaching half a billion people in 137 countries.

Steve Irwin was larger than life—flamboyant, exuberant, and energetic to the max. He wore bush khakis wherever he went, spoke in an exaggerated Aussie accent, and became known for his catchphrase, "Crikey!" Irwin's mission was to bring people and the natural world together, and he did so with infectious enthusiasm.

My friend Garr Reynolds, in his blog Presentation Zen (September 6, 2006), called Steve "a great presenter and teacher" and "a man of action and passion." He quoted Irwin as saying, "I believe that education is all about being excited about something. Seeing passion and enthusiasm helps push an educational message."

In addition to his successful TV career, Irwin was building a film career. He parlayed a cameo in Eddie Murphy's *Dr. Doolittle 2* (2001) into a feature film role, playing

(continued)

himself in the family-friendly spy adventure *The Crocodile Hunter: Collision Course* (2002). Produced for twelve million dollars, the movie grossed thirty-three million.

What was it about the Crocodile Hunter that made millions love him and mourn his passing? "Steve was a great communicator," said Virginia Young, strategic campaign coordinator for the Wilderness Society, "and he was a champion of wild nature. His larrikin style helped build community understanding and deepen appreciation of Australia's unique natural heritage."[5]

His "larrikin style"? I had to look the word up. *Larrikin* means "a person noted for comical, outlandish behavior." In the old dialects of the West Midlands in central England, *larrikin* originally meant "tongue" and was a term applied to people who were "gobby" or "mouthy" and always wagging their tongues in an exuberant, talkative manner. That was Steve Irwin, through and through.

Steve once appeared at an awards ceremony, standing next to Australia's tourism minister Margaret Keech as she gave a rather dry and formal speech. "He thought I was being too serious," Ms. Keech recalled, "so he shouted, 'Crikey!' just to get me laughing! It worked."[6]

The man was a brilliant, uninhibited communicator. He didn't just communicate with his voice and his eyes, but with his whole face. He didn't merely gesture—he threw his whole body into every word he said. He grabbed his audience by the ears, the eyes, and the First Brain, and he didn't let go! He used storytelling, visuals, suspense, and surprise to keep his audience riveted.

Millions of people, young and old, have been converted to the conservationist cause by Steve Irwin's electric zeal and his genuineness. He loved people and never thought of himself as a celebrity. At his zoo, he rode around on a minibike and was available for the visitors to meet and talk to.

Steve Irwin was a larrikinesque Noah who connected with his audiences as few have ever done in any field. Listen to the passion in this CNN interview excerpt: "I have got to be right in there. I have to get right, fierce, smack into the action! Because the day has come where the audience—you!—need to come with me and be there with that animal. If there are whales dying on the beach in western Tasmania, I want to share it with you, because if we can touch people about wildlife then they want to save it!"[7]

When Steve Irwin died at age forty-four, no one could believe he was truly gone. He lived a short, rich life packed with excitement and accomplishment. When he spoke, he connected—and that's why he's loved and missed today.

CHAPTER 2

Emotion Versus Fact

A Living, Breathing Résumé

Christine Figari is a trainer who has worked for Decker Communications for many years. She first called me on the phone when the company was only a couple of years old and quite a bit leaner than it is today. "We're really not hiring new trainers right now but go ahead and send your résumé," I said. "We're always looking for good people."

I was working in my office the next day when my receptionist, Bobbie, brought her résumé in. "I told her you wouldn't be able to talk to her without an appointment," said Bobbie, "but she insists on seeing you in person." I quickly scanned the résumé and saw it was good, but nothing spectacular. I thought this was a little pushy, but figured I ought to at least be friendly, so I walked down the hall. I found Christine to be much more impressive than her résumé.

What really struck me was her certainty—a lot of energy in her voice and her manner, great posture, an authentic smile. She radiated confidence and competence. I learned more of what I needed to know about Chris within the first thirty seconds after we shook hands than from her entire résumé.

We ended up talking for half an hour. Two months later, she was hired.

That's the power of a living, breathing résumé versus the ink-on-paper variety. Chris understood she wasn't just looking for a job; she was selling herself—her skills, her competence, her confidence, her personality. She understood that these are qualities you just can't convey on a piece of paper.

Communication Is Selling

So what are you selling? After all, we're all selling something.

Does that rub you the wrong way? Are you like so many who object to that word *selling*? I hope not. Because every time you and I communicate, we are selling. Some of us sell products. Some of us sell ideas. Some sell a viewpoint. And we all sell ourselves. In every arena of our careers and private lives—management, sales, training, education, politics, church, clubs, home, or cocktail parties—we are engaged in selling something.

In this context, the idea of selling can be used interchangeably with the idea of persuading or reaching agreement. Once we see communication as a form of selling, it suddenly hits home that we had better get serious about communicating *effectively* if we want to be successful, to have some influence, or simply to have others hear and understand us.

So, if communication is selling, then what we want is for our listeners to "buy in," to agree. We want to influence our listeners to make a decision in our favor. And what will our listeners base that decision on? Primarily, on how they feel about us, on information received at an emotional level, on whether we've made emotional contact.

If the first thing to understand about communication is that we are all selling something, then the second and even more crucial thing to understand is this:

PEOPLE BUY ON EMOTION AND JUSTIFY WITH FACT.

You may resist this statement. You may want to shout, "No! No! No! I am a rational, cognitive human being! I make calm, considered, well-thought-out decisions! I do not buy on emotion!"

But I can prove this statement. And I'll show you why it's really the key to effective communication. By the time you've finished this book, I hope you'll have this principle scrawled across your time manager, emblazoned on your desk blotter at work, taped to the dashboard of your car, and posted on your refrigerator at home. Contrary to our academic training, people do buy on emotion and justify with fact. Once we've accepted this basic fact of communication, we can use it to become more effective and persuasive in our own communication.

SUB-, UN-, OR PRECONSCIOUS?

Any attempt to divide and subdivide the mind by the use of semantics is doomed to imprecision. The little that we do know with certainty about the mind tells us that its processes cannot be parsed into neat categories.

Although terms such as *subconscious, unconscious,* and *preconscious* have acquired clinical definitions among psychiatrists and psychologists, most laypeople use these words rather carelessly and interchangeably. Moreover, the words *subconscious* and *unconscious* have acquired connotations from Freud, Jung, and their respective disciples that could easily confuse the issue. So I've chosen to use the word *preconscious*, which seems to be appropriately free of such baggage.

Preconscious means: "Not present in consciousness but capable of being recalled without encountering any inner resistance or repression."

This is a good description of the level of consciousness we are describing when we talk about making emotional contact when we communicate. Our listeners are probably not consciously aware of the nonverbal cues we give that, taken together, shape either a positive or a negative impression of us as speakers. But they are probably preconsciously aware.

Ask a listener, "What was it you liked or disliked about that speaker?" and he or she might pause for a moment to mentally rewind the tape and play back some visual and auditory impressions. Then the listener might reply, "He seemed unsure of himself. He didn't have much confidence in himself or his message. I felt anxious and nervous just listening to him." Or, "She seemed warm and spontaneous. Very relaxed and confident. She held my interest the whole time."

We rarely pause to consciously inspect the state and activity of our preconscious mind. But it is there, all the same, recording impressions, making judgments, and powerfully affecting the communication process.

Here's the proof. Think back to a major decision you made. A big purchase such as a car or house. Your choice of college. Your first job. The person you married. These are major life-affecting decisions, and we all like to think we make such decisions in a fairly (if not completely) rational way.

But let me ask you this: When you were making that big decision, did you take out a yellow legal pad, write *Pro* and *Con* at the top, and make a list of all the reasons for deciding yes or no? Not likely. And if you actually did that, did you then make your choice purely on the basis of the weight of those answers? And what then were the primary, scale-tipping reasons for your decision?

I'm not saying you didn't do research or give the decision a lot of thought. I am saying that most of our major decisions are overwhelmingly influenced at the emotional level, the preconscious level. We in effect decide (or "buy") at that level and then use our intellect to justify our decisions.

When Christine Figari arrived in person at my office—a "living résumé" rather than a dead piece of paper—she established emotional contact with me as a prospective employer, and she closed the sale. As an employer, I "bought" Chris on an emotional basis. I liked her, I was impressed with her, and I knew that the clients of our company, whom she would be training, would like her and be impressed with her too. I'm not sure that I would have "bought" Chris on the factual basis of her résumé alone.

Let me describe a few situations from everyday life to further show you what I mean when I say that people buy on emotion and justify with fact.

TOM LOVES KAYE

Tom and Kaye are getting married. (A true story with names changed.) Tom's a stockbroker, a facts-and-figures, data-oriented kind of guy. Sure, he's in love with Kaye, but he's figured this whole thing out rationally—or so he thinks! Look at his reasons for marrying her: First, she's smart. Then there are her eyes, deep blue with flecks of violet. Of course they get along well and are from the same neighborhood. And then there are those lips with just a hint of a pout. On top of that, Kaye makes an incredible ratatouille Provençale. And she's got a great sense of humor (meaning she laughs at his jokes).

Okay, so Tom's a Republican and Kaye votes Independent. And yes, he's an Episcopalian and she's a not anything. He likes staying home, reading books, working with computers, and listening to golden oldies. She hates typing but likes windsurfing, rock climbing, and New Age/fusion. But according to Tom, they've really got a lot in common.

Right.

JANA LOVES HER HOUSE

Or take another example. Jana, a single woman in her early thirties, is thinking about buying a house. It fits her personality perfectly: cute, a lot of charm, though a little drafty. Jana calmly, unemotionally draws up a ledger of pros and cons:

PRO	CON
It's cute	Wrong neighborhood
It's got charm	Leaky plumbing
L.R. paneling matches my coffee table	Wiring is shot
It's quaint	I can't afford the payments

Okay, she reasons, so the neighborhood's a little run-down. And the place needs some fixing here and there. And the mortgage payments will eat up two-thirds of my take-home pay. No problem. I'll just take peanut butter sandwiches to work instead of eating out. And I'll sell my car and take the bus to work. Maybe I can get a weekend job. With that, Jana arrives at the perfectly rational, unemotional decision that she can afford her dream house.

Right.

Does any of this sound familiar? If you think about it, and if you're honest with yourself, you have to admit that your decisions are often made on the basis of "This is what I want to do." Then you think up all the reasons why what you want to do is really the logical thing to do. We all buy on emotion and justify with fact. All of us. I see it in myself all the time.

DRIVING IT HOME

The car I'm driving right now was bought on emotion.

I like big cars. So when my wife, Dru Scott, and I walked onto the lot, my gaze was immediately arrested by this roomy, classy, all-white Lincoln Town Car. We took it for a test drive, then brought it back to the lot. I wanted that car, but I didn't want to be impulsive. (I'm naturally impulsive, but trying to curb it.)

"What do you think?" the salesman asked eagerly. He knew the hook was set. He was just waiting to reel me in.

"This is my first look," I said, shaking my head. "I need to look at a few other models first. Besides, it's really more than I'd planned to spend."

The salesman's face sagged. We got in my old car and started to drive off. Before we had gone half a block, Dru turned and with an understanding smile said, "You really like that car, don't you?"

That's all I needed. I grinned, spun the wheel, whipped back into the lot, and *bought* that big beautiful car, just like that. I still like that car. It was a good decision. But it was an *emotional* decision.

The fact that we buy on emotion is *a natural* fact, neither good nor bad. Sometimes buying on emotion gets us into trouble—the kind of trouble—Tom and Jana are headed for. And then, sometimes we get lucky, as I did when I bought that car. An emotional decision isn't necessarily the wrong decision.

There's no shame in admitting we're emotional creatures, and that emotion has a powerful driving influence on everything we do, think, and choose. In fact, it's foolish not to admit it. The truth is, if you want to reach, persuade, or motivate people, you have to make emotional contact with them.

AMERICA VOTES ON EMOTION

John F. Kennedy was a political leader who knew how to make emotional contact with his audience. A few weeks before the debates, Kennedy trailed Nixon in the polls, 47 percent to 53 percent. By election day, Kennedy had not only caught up with, but nosed ahead of Nixon. Historians attribute Kennedy's narrow 1960 victory over Richard Nixon to their televised debates—a view shared by Kennedy himself, who said, "It was TV more than anything else that turned the tide." It was generally agreed that Richard Nixon (like Mondale and Dukakis in later debates) won the debates on radio. He won on debating points. Yet it was Kennedy who emerged victorious among TV viewers.[1]

When Nixon arrived at the Chicago television studio for the first debate, he was haggard and drawn-looking because of intense campaigning combined with a recent hospitalization for a knee injury from which he had not yet fully recovered. He had lost twenty pounds and was not feeling well. He had spent five hours stuffing his head with answers to potential questions.

During the debate, he sweated profusely under the studio lights, streaking the pallid "lazy shave" makeup that was supposed to hide the deep five o'clock shadow on his jowls. Even though Nixon's discussion of the issues was cogent, and his grasp of events and factual detail was authoritative, all the viewers could recall of the debates was the image of a candidate who perspired under pressure, whose eyes darted during questioning, who seemed to lack confidence and poise.

In the debates and on the campaign stump, Nixon tried to appeal on the basis of facts, records, and statistics. As one historian observes, "Nixon constantly emphasized his superiority over Kennedy in experience, expressing it in the form of statistics. He had had 173 meetings with Ike, he said, and 217 with the National Security Council, over which he had presided 26 times. He had attended 163 cabinet meetings, presiding over 19. He had visited 54 countries, with extended discussions with 35 presidents, 9 prime ministers, 2 emperors, and the Shah of Iran."[2]

Dissecting the Nixon Debacle

On September 26, 1960, the CBS television network preempted *The Andy Griffith Show* in order to present the first of four televised debates between Richard Nixon and John F. Kennedy. Carried live from Chicago, the first debate was seen by an audience of seventy million people. For Old Communicator Nixon, it was an unmitigated disaster. While his opponent skillfully used the new visual medium of television to make emotional contact with the audience, Nixon found himself impaled by its penetrating rays.

Dissecting the Nixon debacle in her book *Richard Nixon: The Shaping of His Character,* Fawn Brodie commented, "Those who missed the television and heard Nixon and Kennedy only on radio thought Nixon had clearly bested his opponent. But many television viewers who saw the Nixon pallor, the trickle of sweat pouring down his chin, the struggle to overcome his discomfiture at the Vanocur question [regarding an embarrassing remark about Nixon by President Eisenhower], remembered very little else. Nixon's running mate, Henry Cabot Lodge, watching the debate on TV in Texas, blurted out . . . when the debate was over, 'That son-of-a-bitch just lost us the election!' "

Nixon's on-screen appearance was so alarming, Brodie noted, that "Hannah Nixon [Nixon's mother] called Rose Woods in dismay to ask if her son was ill, and a disturbed Pat Nixon immediately took a plane from Washington to Chicago." Barry Goldwater called the debates "a disaster," and *The New Republic* concluded, "The debates ruined Nixon."

Nixon mistakenly thought the audience would build, debate by debate. Instead, the audience fell by twenty million after the first disastrous outing. It's inconclusive but intriguing to speculate that the reason those twenty million viewers tuned out was that they had already made up their minds after Nixon's initial performance.

Eight years later a "New Nixon" emerged, reshaped and reanimated by Roger Ailes, the man who later coached the debate and campaign performances of New Communicators Ronald Reagan and George H. W. Bush. The New Nixon learned to smile. He played to the crowds and to the unblinking eye of TV. The New Nixon was visual and energetic, employing such visual tactics as standing on the hood of a limousine and flashing V for victory. The New Nixon showed us a lighter side, appearing on Rowan and Martin's *Laugh-In* to pose the burning question, "Sock it to me?"

The New Nixon of course won the presidency in 1968 and 1972. Then the habits of the Old Communicator crept back in as Nixon stonewalled the Congress, the press, and the public during the Watergate scandal. The rest is history.

Statistics are cold and cerebral. And so, the nation concluded, was Richard Nixon. America wanted emotional contact with its leader. JFK was happy to oblige.

Kennedy arrived for the first debate looking calm, assured, and dashing. In contrast to Nixon's "lazy shave" pallor, Kennedy was tanned from a recent campaign swing through California. On-screen, he was animated and totally in control. Whereas Nixon radiated edginess and anxiety, Kennedy communicated in a natural, relaxed style that Cold War–weary voters found reassuring.

In those early days of television, almost as many people heard the debate on radio or read it in newsprint as saw it on TV, so the impact of TV was not as great as it might have been in our video-saturated world of the 1990s. Kennedy, who was trailing in the polls before the debate, just squeaked by Nixon with a scant 112,000-vote margin out of more than 68,800,000 votes cast. Had the video technology of the 1980s and 1990s been around in 1960, I think it's safe to say that Kennedy would have buried Nixon in a landslide.

Kennedy won because—either consciously or intuitively—he understood how to make *emotional contact* with his audience. Election results have comparatively little to do with a candidate's intelligence, managerial skill, position papers, or party affiliation. Sure, they count, they're important, but you have to have something else first: *human contact* with the decision maker—the voter. Election results are more profoundly influenced by the question "Which candidate do I trust?" than by any other issue. This is an emotional question. When America chooses its leaders, it buys on emotion and justifies with fact.

MY $450,000 MISTAKE

I didn't understand this concept years ago, and it cost me dearly. I was a producer-director of documentary and political films. When the National Park Service put a major $450,000 film contract out for bids, my film company went after it with a vengeance. We had a good record of past work with the Park Service, and this was *a big* contract. After writing the proposal, we knew it was good. The ideas were innovative. Our credentials were solid. This should've been a winner. And sure enough, out of the hundreds of proposals submitted, ours was among the three finalists.

My friend Carl Degen was on the five-person committee that would make the decision. He had told me our written proposal was tied for the lead. The committee then flew me and the two other producers to Washington, D.C., for an interview. I remember sitting at a table with the committee for an hour, talking about our film concepts and answering questions. Then I went back to the hotel and waited through the afternoon for the committee's decision.

Finally, the phone rang. It was Carl. "Sorry, Bert, I hate to be the one to tell you that you lost."

"But why?" I said, disbelieving. "The proposal was great! Carl, you even told me we were in the lead with the written concepts! What went wrong?"

There was a long hesitation, then Carl said, "Bert, you looked nervous."

I remember thinking, *That's not right! It shouldn't matter if a guy is nervous in an interview, so long as he can deliver quality goods, on time and on budget. Besides, it was a high-pressure situation—he could be expected to be nervous.* "Unfair!" I said then.

But now I would just say, "Of course!" On paper, at the "facts" level, our proposal and our company looked great. But in person, I blew it. My words were okay, but I sent out a message that registered on an emotional level. It was *a silent* message—perhaps consisting of poor eye communication, fidgety gestures, and the like—but those silent cues *screamed* that I lacked self-confidence. My visible nervousness undermined my message and the committee's trust in me. It was a $450,000 lesson, but an important one. For that was when I found out that people buy on emotion and justify with fact.

CHAPTER 3

Your Personal Impact

"Chuck, You Need Help"

Charles R. Schwab launched his company in 1971, pioneering the concept of a discount brokerage and opening the stock market to the masses. In the 1990s, seeing the power of the Internet, Chuck Schwab invented a whole new approach to stock ownership: online trading. Today, the Charles Schwab Corporation provides financial services to over seven million accounts. Today, Chuck is not only the CEO, but the company's very public spokesman and center of the "Talk To Chuck" advertising campaign. Today, his company is listed in the top 50 of the Forbes 400, and his net worth is estimated at $4.6 billion.

In the early 1980s, Chuck's business was booming—but he was facing some difficult news. He and his wife, Helen, were taking their son through a lengthy and frustrating assessment process because of problems he was having in school. Finally, the diagnosis came back. Their son was dyslexic. The Schwabs knew very little about dyslexia at the time, but as they met with their son's school psychologist, a major revelation dawned. Chuck realized that the problems his son had

Charles Schwab

with reading and writing mirrored the problems he himself had experienced all through school and into his adult life.

Chuck realized that he was dyslexic too. At that moment, he entered an entirely new phase of his life.

"As a kid I was good at a lot of things," he explains, "but I could never remember in sequence. It goes back to the fact that I was dyslexic. When I was younger, no one knew how to diagnose dyslexia. No one knew what my problem was. I just knew there were things I couldn't do that other kids could do with ease, such as memorizing a passage of poetry. In those days they taught public speaking by rote, by memorization. So I had no confidence in that area and was unable to get up and speak in front of people."

Charles Schwab wasn't a poor student. As a child he exhibited the mental acuity and talent that would one day make him one of America's top executives. But because of an undiagnosed problem that hampered his ability to decode and use language, he was slow in sequential thinking and reading while excelling in abstract thinking. Unfortunately, abstract thinking wasn't rewarded in the school system—and it still isn't today.

From his youth on into adulthood, Charles Schwab shunned public speaking because he felt inadequate in front of an audience. Though he was successful in business, he knew that his lack of confidence and communicating skill was holding him back from far greater success— yet he didn't know what to do about it.

At around the same time Schwab and his son were both diagnosed with dyslexia, one of the officers in his company took him aside and said something that stunned and angered him. "He was one of my most trusted officers," Chuck recalls. "He'd been with me since the beginning. He came up to me and said, 'Chuck, you need help. You need to be up-front, representing the company—and to do that, you need to improve your public speaking skills.' I was amazed and frankly a little upset. Here we had just reached our dream, we were on a new plateau and had just gotten the backing to expand our business—and suddenly I was being criticized!

"But after I got over my initial defensiveness, I realized he was right.

If we were to succeed at this new higher-profile level, I did need help in becoming more of a public figure. We had used still photos extensively in our advertising campaigns, but I had always shied away from any speaking engagements. My friend was telling me it was time to change, time to go to the next level."

And Charles Schwab did change. He came to my company and we showed him an entirely new way of communicating. It was an approach that even worked well with his dyslexia. Everything he learned, you are about to learn in these very pages.

I don't have to tell you about the transformation in my friend Charles Schwab. You've seen him in his company's commercials and on live TV interview shows. You can also find him in front of an audience, looking relaxed and confident. Public speaking isn't his most enjoyable pastime, but he excels at it and he knows he's effective as a speaker. And by stepping in front of the TV cameras as the believable, likable, persuasive face of the Charles Schwab Corporation, he has taken the company—and his own fortunes—to levels of success he scarcely dreamed of back in the 1980s.

In fact, Charles Schwab's personal impact is so important to the company that the latest Schwab ad campaign is called "Talk to Chuck." In this campaign, he looks his audience right in the eye and says, "I'm Chuck Schwab, and I believe that when you look for someone you can trust with your hard-earned money, your kids' money, or your grandkids' money, it all comes down to this: Who can you talk to?" Chuck Schwab is likable and trustworthy—and the company was smart to build a campaign around his personal impact. He connects at the emotional level.

And Chuck Schwab isn't just one of the wealthiest, most successful people in America. He's also one of the most caring and empathetic. His own experience has given him a heart for helping others with dyslexia. "My son is dyslexic and my sister is dyslexic," he says. "We set up the Charles and Helen Schwab Foundation to help dyslexic kids and their parents. These kids need parents who are trained to understand, accept, and deal with the problem. They need to know that, even though they struggle with learning, they're not stupid and they can learn and feel great about themselves if they have the right tools. And the parents need their own support, too."

Through the foundation, Chuck has founded Schwab Learning (visit SchwabLearning.org), a resource center providing information and support for families with learning disability issues. Chuck and Helen Schwab are using their experiences and resources to help kids with dyslexia and other learning disabilities to succeed in life—and one of the ways Chuck supports these organizations is through his skills as a public speaker.

Charles R. Schwab was not always a natural communicator. But today he's a New Communicator, one of the most effective speakers on the American business scene. Why? Because he made a decision to do something about his personal impact.

And because a friend cared enough to tell him, "Chuck, you need help."

Are You a Public Speaker?

How do you answer this question in your own mind? It's a question I frequently ask when I speak before large groups: "How many of you are public speakers?" Even in a room of a thousand people, I rarely see more than a dozen or so hands go up. So I say, "How many of you are private speakers—or would like to be?" A lot of laughs on that one.

The point is clear: We are *all* public speakers. There's no such thing as a "private speaker" (except a person who talks to himself—and you don't want to be one of those!). Every person who talks to another person is a public speaker. You and I are continually in the public eye, selling our products, our ideas, ourselves, all of the time.

As you can see, *public speaking* means a lot more than merely "giving speeches." We're talking about your *personal* impact. We're talking about your ability to connect emotionally with others whenever you have something to say.

Many people mistakenly think that one's personal impact, the impression one makes, comes primarily from external factors: an appealing face, an attractive physique, stylish clothes. These are all important features of your personal presence, to be sure—but they are not the most important factors in the personal impact you have on others.

Even if nature hasn't blessed you with movie star good looks, even if you are a little too thin or a little too portly, you can wow an audience with your confidence, your believability, and your likability. Your personal impact doesn't come primarily from your looks, but from your behavior. Let me give you an example.

One of the most effective and successful public speakers in America is a big, moon-faced teddy bear of a man who owes his 250-pound frame to a hankering for mint chocolate chip ice cream. His favorite TV show is *America's Funniest Home Videos*. Physically, he resembles NBC's jovial weatherman Willard Scott or even comedian Jonathan Winters. Even his name sounds kind of funny: Norman Schwarzkopf.

But as the commander of Operation Desert Storm during the first Gulf War in 1991, "Stormin' Norman" Schwarzkopf was Saddam Hussein's worst nightmare. After that war, General Schwarzkopf became a symbol of American achievement and the American spirit at its best.

Why? Not just because he won the war, but also because of the way he could communicate to an audience. Norman Schwarzkopf connects with his listeners, powerfully and persuasively. He reaches the emotions of our First Brain.

We first saw his public speaking skills on display during his historic strategy briefing at the conclusion of the Gulf War in February 1991. This press conference (where he revealed the "Hail Mary" surprise plan that routed the enemy) was so memorable it soon became a hot-selling videocassette.

In May 1991, Schwarzkopf made an encore appearance before an emotionally charged joint session of Congress. His speech was interrupted dozens of times by standing ovations. He spoke for only sixteen and a half minutes—and he spent over a third of that time waiting for applause to subside.

With passion, he spoke of the pride of the American soldier: "We're the United States military, and we're damn proud of it!" There was a catch in his throat as he paid tribute to the fallen. His eyes glistened, his voice choked, and he cast a sentimental smile toward his wife and

Norman Schwarzkopf (TERRY ASHE/TIME & LIFE PICTURES/GETTY IMAGES)

children in the gallery as he said, "We also want to thank the families. . . . It was your love that truly gave us strength in our darkest hours." His expression flashed with hot, righteous indignation as he excoriated "the prophets of doom, the naysayers, and the flag burners."

Schwarzkopf climaxed his address with a rolling refrain: "Thank you, America! Thank you, America! Thank you to the great people of the United States of America!" It was a star-quality speech by a man who hardly gave the appearance of a granite-jawed Hollywood hero. Yet he connected with his audience, and he was applauded as a hero. In the months that followed, his ability to communicate made him a very rich hero.

Schwarzkopf retired from the military in August 1991 and wrote his autobiography, *It Doesn't Take a Hero,* published in 1992. He went on a speaking tour to promote the book, and it sold more than a million copies in hardcover and remained on the *New York Times* Best Seller List for twenty-five weeks.

In retirement, General Schwarzkopf has served as a military analyst and continues to use his speaking skills to promote awareness of prostate cancer (he underwent successful treatment for the disease in 1993). Fifteen years after the end of the first Gulf War, he still commands a fee of more than fifty thousand dollars for a single speech. If a portly, moon-faced teddy bear like Norman Schwarzkopf can be an effective public speaker, so can you.

Personal impact is power—the power to achieve whatever you want in your life and your career. The secret of attaining personal impact is based on three fundamental truths:

Truth Number 1
The spoken word is almost the polar opposite of the written word.

Truth Number 2
In the spoken medium, what you say must be believed to have impact.

Truth Number 3
Believability is overwhelmingly determined at a preconscious level.

Let's look at each of these transformational truths in turn.

TRUTH NUMBER 1: WRITING ISN'T SPEAKING, AND VICE VERSA

The spoken word and the written word are not just different ways of using words. They are completely different forms of communicating.

Written communication is linear, single-channel input. We receive it through our eyes alone. We take in written communication word by word and line by line.

Spoken communication, by contrast, is multichannel input. In spoken communication, the message we receive is not merely a row of words, but also a kaleidoscopic array of nonverbal cues.

The information channel. If all you want to do is transfer information, don't say it, put it in writing. Written communication is much more effective than speaking for exchanging facts, data, and details. You can read five times faster than a person can speak. You can go back and reread for a clearer understanding. You can concentrate on content and ignore the nuances. You can skim it, file it for later reference, fax it, or e-mail it. Written communication is the "information channel," and it definitely has its place.

But if your goal is to influence, to persuade, to get your point across, then you've got to say it—and say it with impact. You've got to use the action channel, not the information channel.

The action channel. Writing is like a monaural recording: the message comes through on only one channel. Speaking, however, is like a multichannel Surround Sound experience, in which dozens of channels simultaneously feed information to the human mind. These various channels communicate a richly textured, multilayered message from speaker to listener. These channels consist of:

- Posture
- Facial expression
- Energy level

- Eye communication
- Vocal inflection
- Vocal intonation
- Volume
- Gestures and other physical actions
- And more

These channels are nonverbal cues that accompany and modify the words of the message. The human mind relies more heavily than most of us realize on these nonverbal channels as a means of decoding the spoken message. In fact, the mind attributes far more importance to these nonverbal cues than it does to the actual words that are spoken.

Written communication goes directly to the cerebral cortex, the highly developed reasoning and analytical portion of the brain. Spoken communication carries energy, feeling, and passion and goes straight to the emotional center of the brain—what I call the First Brain. It is this emotional side that we have to reach if we want to motivate and persuade people because, as we've already seen, people generally buy on emotion—not on fact, reason, or analysis.

I would guess that about 80 percent of the average person's communication falls into the category of speaking to persuade. This is action-oriented communication. It takes place not only in speeches on a platform, but in presentations, in meetings, in across-the-desk discussions, in informal chats over lunch, and on the golf course. It takes place at church, at home, at the car dealership, in small claims court, and at yard sales.

Once we've grasped the crucial fact that writing and speaking are completely different ways of communicating, it becomes clear that the job of selling ourselves, our ideas, and our products should not just be committed to writing. If we want to convince and motivate others, we must say it with impact.

If you want the boss to give you a raise, don't send him a memo. Go to his office, look him in the eye, and persuade him that you're worth it.

If you want to sell that client on your product, don't write her a letter. Get into her office and persuade her that she's got to have your product.

If you're looking for a job, don't mail out résumés like so much junk mail. Get into that employer's office and persuade him you're the only person for the job.

Most of us are like Tony, a bank computer analyst I trained in our two-day program. Tony was a bright guy with a logical mind, a wizard with computers, and an effective writer. He had just been promoted to manager, and his company had told him to take the training. He did so—but grudgingly.

Tony resisted almost every exercise we did during the first morning. He didn't like speaking extemporaneously. He didn't like being video-taped so that he could see his own performance. More than once, he asked, "What are we doing this for?" We usually win people over very quickly in the course, but Tony was a tough case. Out of a dozen participants, he was the only holdout.

Just before lunch on the first day, I talked to the group about speaking versus writing. Tony looked skeptical. "I'm sorry, Bert," he said, "but I just don't buy it. Writing and speaking are just two ways of doing the same thing. Words on paper or words in the air, what's the difference? To me, communicating is very simple. You can either say it or you can write it, but once it's been heard or read by someone else, it's communicated, period."

"Tony," I said, "do me a favor. Stay with us, go through the exercises, listen to everything we say. When it's all over, if you still feel the same way, you get your money back."

After lunch we did impromptu exercises. We videotaped the participants as they tried new communicating skills. Then, in private coaching sessions, I worked individually with the participants, reviewing their taped performances. When Tony's turn came, we went into the coaching room, rolled the tape, and compared Tony's morning performance with his afternoon performance. Tony was amazed at what he saw. Even with his skepticism cranked full blast, even with all his foot-dragging and doubting, he had made visible progress.

In the afternoon tapings, he looked more relaxed, confident, and natural. He saw that he could get up before a group, make an emotional connection, and actually be persuasive, likable, believable, and completely himself. "Incredible," he said. "I'm amazed at the difference."

Later, Tony got up before the group and said, "You all know I've been resistant to everything we've been doing. I still don't want to believe that speaking is any different from writing, but I can't deny it anymore. I've seen the proof on video. What makes this hard for me is that I've got to change my whole way of thinking."

Tony put his finger on it: *We've got to change our whole way of thinking about communicating!* It means changing some stubborn and deeply grooved habits. It means dumping old mental programming and inserting new. It means shedding comfortable but self-defeating behavior patterns.

Revising our thinking is one of the hardest things human beings have to do. But because you're reading this book, I'm confident that you—unlike my friend Tony—won't need to be dragged kicking and screaming to this inescapable conclusion: *Writing and speaking are totally different and opposed ways of communicating.*

The facts are clear: If you merely want to transfer data, put it in writing. But if you need to motivate, persuade, and influence people, *say it with impact.*

> Faced with the choice between changing one's mind and proving there is no need to do so, almost everyone gets busy on the proof.
>
> John Kenneth Galbraith

TRUTH NUMBER 2: YOU'VE GOT TO BE BELIEVED TO BE HEARD

In the spoken medium, what you say must be believed in order to have impact. No message, regardless of how eloquently stated, brilliantly defended, and painstakingly documented, can penetrate a wall of distrust, apprehension, or indifference. If you want to persuade, you must be believed. And to be believed, you must be believable. A listener who doesn't trust you and find you believable will not even hear what you have to say.

TRUTH NUMBER 3: BELIEF IS DETERMINED AT A PRECONSCIOUS LEVEL

Where does believability come from?

You can't build believability out of a mountain of facts and figures. You can't even build it out of stacks of elegantly crafted words. Authoritative credentials—a big accomplishment, a title, or a Ph.D.— may buy you some credibility, but only enough to get your foot in the door. You still have to come across as believable in order to "close the sale."

Believability is an emotional quality. It's built on an emotional (First Brain) level, not a rational and cognitive level.

Let's say you're attending a national sales meeting. You're in an auditorium with five hundred other people from your company. The first speaker is introduced and there is a round of applause. He steps to the podium, adjusts his glasses, fumbles with a sheaf of pages, and begins reading his speech. His eyes are downcast. His voice is high and tremulous with tension. After a seeming eternity, he reaches the end of page one. The microphone picks up the nervous rattle of the paper as he turns to page two.

You groan inwardly and tune out. You flip to the back of your printed agenda and check the speaker's credentials. *And I was looking forward to hearing this guy,* you say to yourself. *It says here he's an expert, but he sure doesn't seem too confident of his material.*

Now the speaker really *is* an expert in his field. Too bad he appears to lack conviction and enthusiasm. Just this morning, he was talking about this very same subject with a colleague. He was full of excitement, he was expressive, he was confident. One-on-one, he's natural and believable. But put him behind a lectern and he's a sure cure for insomnia. At most, maybe 5 percent of his content gets through to the audience.

The next speaker is introduced. She uses graphics with bold colors and forceful images. She has a strong, distinctive voice, with a wide dynamic range. Instead of planting herself behind the lectern, she moves freely about the platform, making eye contact around the room.

She has an interesting smile and open gestures. She's talking about financial projections (you thought this was going to be a yawner) yet you find yourself listening. You even find yourself feeling enthusiastic about financial projections, and laughing at the speaker's wry asides.

Coffee-break time. You chat with your associates. You meet a new sales rep. You shake his hand—oops, limp and clammy! And the guy looks so grim. How did he ever get hired? You're not conscious of it, but he's actually sending out additional nonverbal cues through his posture, eye contact, voice, and other signals, all of which add up to a negative impression. He sends these same cues when he calls on accounts. In a few months, he'll be history.

And so it goes. Throughout the meeting, you've been bombarded with literally thousands of stimuli—the sights, sounds, and personal energy of speakers, colleagues, superiors, subordinates, friends, and new acquaintances. And these people have received a similar array of verbal and nonverbal cues from *you*.

An enormous amount of communication is taking place as these thousands of multichannel impressions are carried to your brain. Most of these impressions register at a preconscious level. As a result of these impressions, your brain forms a continuous stream of emotional judgments and assessments, answering questions like Do I trust this person? Is he or she honest? Evasive? Friendly? Threatening? Interesting? Boring? Warm? Cold? Anxious? Confident? Insecure? Hiding something?

The emotional judgments formed in your preconscious mind about the speaker determine whether you will tune in to the message—or tune out.

If you don't believe in someone on an emotional level, little of that person's message will get through. It will be screened out by your distrust, your anxiety, your irritation, or your indifference. Even if the facts and content are great by themselves, they are forever locked out because the person delivering them lacks believability.

You really do have to be believed to be heard.

A Tale of Two Yalies

My favorite singing group? The Whiffenpoofs. Favorite Cole Porter tune? "Bulldog! Bulldog! Bow Wow Wow!" Favorite color? Yale blue. That's right, I'm a true-blue Eli—a Yale grad.

Now here's a bit of historical trivia: As this book goes to press, there's been at least one Yale alum on a major-party ticket in every presidential election since 1972. That's right. Gerald R. Ford, George H. W. Bush, George W. Bush, Bill Clinton, Sargent Shriver, Joseph Lieberman, Dick Cheney, and John Kerry were all Yalies.

I opened this book with an examination of Yale grad George W. Bush—a president who, despite flashes of communicating greatness, has let himself and the nation down by not speaking more often and more effectively. Now let's compare and contrast Mr. Bush with a fellow Yalie and one of the most skilled communicators in the history of the White House: William Jefferson Clinton.

When Bill Clinton speaks, people listen. Whether you love him or hate him, you have to admit that Mr. Clinton is a master communicator. One Clinton detractor, Senator George Voinovich (R-Ohio), voted to remove Mr. Clinton from office during the impeachment proceedings of 1999—yet even in his impeachment statement, Voinovich called Mr. Clinton "a very popular, brilliant communicator with extraordinary interpersonal skills."

Clinton's admirers also cite his amazing ability as a communicator. Brian Wolff, political director for House Speaker Nancy Pelosi, told *Washington Life* magazine that Mr. Clinton is "the most brilliant communicator of our generation . . . the Democrat most feared by Republicans for good reason—period."[1]

In terms of education, Bill Clinton is an anomaly. He learned most of his communicating skills outside of traditional academia—and that's probably why he's such an effective communicator. Traditional speech classes at the secondary level teach you to organize content, to articulate, to enunciate, to inform—but they don't teach you how to inspire and connect with your audience. Mr. Bush's stiff, stationary, content-focused approach represents the academic "speech class" approach. Mr. Clinton's

Bill Clinton (CHRISTOPHER FURLONG/GETTY IMAGES)

relaxed manner, movement around the stage, and free use of gestures show that he's much more focused on persuading and connecting than on merely informing.

Bill Clinton loves to talk to audiences. Michael Waldman, who served as chief speechwriter in the Clinton White House, said that Mr. Clinton averaged 550 speeches in a typical nonelection year. Compare that figure with the yearly average of "the Great Communicator," Ronald Reagan (320), or with Harry Truman's paltry 80 speeches per year.[2]

And what about George W. Bush? I picked the nonelection year 2005 and checked his speaking schedule on the WhiteHouse.gov Web site. He had about 290 speaking appearances for the entire year—and that includes all speeches in front of audiences, *plus* roundtable discussions, *plus* press conferences, *plus* I even threw in Mr. Bush's weekly radio addresses. Any way you slice it, Mr. Bush is about half the communicator that Mr. Clinton is.

George W. Bush (MANDEL NGAN/AFP/GETTY IMAGES)

Six years into the Bush presidency, the president's approval ratings were in the mid-30s. Six years into the Clinton presidency, Mr. Clinton's approval ratings were—well, let me quote CNN.com from December 20, 1998: "In the wake of the House of Representatives' approval of two articles of impeachment, Bill Clinton's approval rating has jumped 10 points to 73 percent, the latest CNN/*USA Today*/Gallup poll shows. That's not only an all-time high for Clinton, it also beats the highest approval rating President Ronald Reagan ever had."[3]

Unbelievable! Bill Clinton was facing impeachment. The sordid details of his affair with an intern were well known. So was the fact that he had lied under oath about the matter. *Yet his approval ratings were soaring!* Why? Because Bill Clinton communicated with the American people. Whatever his private failings, Mr. Clinton succeeded in convincing people that he was believable, competent, and trustworthy in matters of public policy, the economy, and other aspects of his job. In speech after speech, in a multitude of public appearances and interviews, he made his *personal impact* felt. He made an emotional connection with the American people—

And the people did not want to see him removed from office.

Bill Clinton survived many obstacles that would have destroyed any other president—Whitewater, Travelgate, Filegate, Paula Jones, and Monica Lewinsky. He not only survived, he thrived. Why? Because he communicated and connected with the American people as no politician has done before or since.

Whether giving a formal speech or in one-on-one settings, Mr. Clinton may well be the most brilliant and effective communicator of our time. Those who have met him say that his persona dominates the room. All who shake hands with him feel—if only for those few moments—that Mr. Clinton is totally focused on them. He makes individuals and audiences feel as if he personally cares about them and their needs.

Perhaps because he grew up poor and fatherless in the South, Mr. Clinton makes a special connection with those who feel downtrodden, discriminated against, and marginalized. Columnist and former Nixon speechwriter William Safire once observed in *The New York Times,* "A pulpit in a black church brings out the best in Clinton."[4]

Many people think that Bill Clinton is just naturally effective as a public speaker. Well, Mr. Clinton undoubtedly has some natural talent as a speaker, but he's also worked hard and practiced many years to hone his communicating skills. In case you doubt that, I'll prove it to you.

Do you remember the performance of then Governor Bill Clinton of Arkansas at the 1988 Democratic National Convention in Atlanta? He was supposed to introduce the party's nominee, Michael Dukakis, and he was told, "Keep it short—no more than fifteen minutes." Clinton couldn't help himself. He gave a meandering, disorganized, yawn-inducing speech that had party leaders in a panic. After thirty minutes, convention aides started turning the house lights on and off. They even flashed the message "Time's up!" on the teleprompter.

Finally, party leader Jim Wright ordered that the mechanical podium on which Clinton stood be lowered. When Bill Clinton felt the platform moving beneath his feet, he finally brought his long-winded "introduction" to a close. After that widely criticized disaster, Mr. Clinton learned to deliver better organized, more concise speeches.

Mr. Clinton also had to learn some new communicating habits—and unlearn some old ones. Early in his 1992 presidential campaign, his advisors noticed that he had a tendency to underscore his most passionate points by wagging his finger at the audience. Finger-pointing makes people feel they are being lectured and scolded. So his advisors came up with a new gesture: a fist held out chest-high, thumb pointed up. Whenever Clinton felt like finger-wagging, he made the "thumbs-up" gesture instead. This distinctive move became so much a part of Mr. Clinton's image that impersonators (such as Darrell Hammond of *Saturday Night Live*) adopted it as a "classic Clinton" gesture.

The thumbs-up movement was learned behavior, not something Bill Clinton did naturally. It made him appear determined yet also warm and likable. There were two notable moments, however, when Mr. Clinton reverted to finger-pointing. One was when he angrily told the news media, "I did not have sexual relations with that woman, Ms. Lewinsky."

The other was during an emotionally charged September 2006 interview with Chris Wallace of Fox News, when Mr. Clinton angrily accused Wallace of doing a "nice little conservative hit job on me."

For Bill Clinton, such slips are rare. In almost every communication setting, he is an absolute paragon of personal impact. Every aspect of his communicating presence is focused on making an emotional connection with his listeners. Here are some of the ways he excels at creating believability and trust:

Appearance: Mr. Clinton makes an immaculate first impression. In speaking situations, he is always well styled and impeccably dressed.

Movement: Bill Clinton pioneered an approach to speaking that has since been adopted by many politicians. To put it simply, he moves around the stage. Traditionally, political speeches always took place behind the barrier of a lectern. Mr. Clinton was the first politician to remove the barrier and use *all* of the stage, including the sides and edges. By moving closer to his audience, Mr. Clinton makes himself seem more accessible and relaxed, less remote.

Impressive Entry. When Bill Clinton enters a room or takes the stage, he instantly commands attention. In fact, at speaking engagements, the audience is usually told to rise when he enters. That note of formality adds to his aura as he takes the podium. You and I may not be able to command presidential respect, but we can find ways to command attention: theme music, PowerPoint visuals, a smile and a wave, anything that will electrify the moment and magnify your personal presence.

Confident Behavior. Mr. Clinton uses a smile, confident body language, a firm stride, and eye communication to send out waves of charisma and self-assurance.

Humor. Mr. Clinton knows how to make an audience laugh, and he often uses self-deprecating humor to good effect. On one occasion, he looked back on his long-winded speech for Dukakis at the 1988 convention and said, "It wasn't my finest hour. It wasn't even my finest hour and a half."

"Fo-shizzle, Ica-zizzle!"

When Lee Iacocca appeared in Chrysler ads in 1981, critics called it an act of desperation, doomed to fail. Some pointed to the failed Eastern Airlines ad campaign featuring company chairman and former astronaut Frank Borman. What the critics didn't understand was that Borman was not a New Communicator. Lee Iacocca was—

And he still is.

In *The Iacocca Management Technique,* auto industry watcher Maynard Gordon wrote about Lee Iacocca's personal impact and believability:

> Chrysler sales rose steadily as more and more Iacocca spots appeared during prime-time dramas, during major athletic events, and between segments of the morning news shows. Chrysler surveys showed that new-car buyers who had ducked Chrysler products for years or had never visited a Chrysler showroom became "converts" as a result of the "credibility" [believability]—an almost indefinable quality—embodied in Iacocca's assertion, "If You Can Find a Better Car, Buy One."
>
> The messages were upbeat and blunt, pitching the products and the company, rapping the competition, daring the viewers or readers to visit Chrysler dealerships and compare them against GM or Ford. . . . A surprisingly large number of Chrysler product buyers . . . said it was belief in Iacocca's message and sincerity that motivated their purchase.

Lee Iacocca often wrote his own ad copy, which enabled him to deliver his lines with genuine conviction. One of the most effective Iacocca ads was his famous "Made in

(continued)

Storytelling. Mr. Clinton has a treasury of anecdotes to draw upon, and he uses them well. His stories (such as his boyhood encounter with President Kennedy at the White House) give his persona a mythic quality that helps to magnify his image and endear him to his audience.

A Call to Involvement. Mr. Clinton often speaks at political events, charitable fund-raisers, and international conferences. He always ends with an appeal for the audience to take action and join a cause. He doesn't just speak to make noise. He speaks to motivate, persuade, and get results.

(continued)

America" commercial. It began on this startlingly straightforward note: "There was a time when 'Made in America' meant something. It meant you made the best. Unfortunately, a lot of Americans don't believe that anymore. And maybe with good reason."

Iacocca proved that the ability to communicate effectively is a multibillion-dollar make-or-break factor. As Maynard Gordon concludes, "No other senior auto executive at the time could communicate . . . with Iacocca's flair for color and candor. . . . The Iacocca persona was, and still is, an irresistible force propelling Chrysler."[5]

Amazingly, more than two decades have passed—and Iacocca is still pitching for Chrysler! The company called him out of retirement in 2005, and eighty-year-old Iacocca made a series of Chrysler commercials that proved he hadn't lost his touch. The first few commercials paired Iacocca with former *Seinfeld* star Jason Alexander. Then came a commercial with nine-year-old child star Naelee Rae, who played his granddaughter. Finally, he did several golf-themed commercials with rapper Snoop Dogg, whose lines included the memorable "Fo-shizzle, Ica-zizzle!" (Translation: "You're absolutely correct, Mr. Iacocca!").

Lee Iacocca's fee was one million dollars plus one dollar for every Chrysler sold, to be donated to his favorite diabetes research charity. The Iacocca ads were a huge success, sending Chrysler sales surging 27 percent higher during the first month of the campaign. The *Detroit News* observed, "Despite being retired from Chrysler for a dozen years, Iacocca still commands the spotlight like no other celebrity CEO ever has."[6]

Now *that's* personal impact!

Now, to conclude this exercise in "compare and contrast," let's take a final look at these two Yalies who have occupied the Oval Office. Bill Clinton loves to talk, loves audiences, and loves to connect with people. George W. Bush speaks when he must, but prefers to run the country from behind a desk. Bill Clinton: 550 speeches a year. George W. Bush: 290 speeches a year. Bill Clinton: a 73 percent approval rating six years into his presidency. George W. Bush: a 35 percent approval rating at around the same point.

As businessman-politician Bruce Barton said so well, "Talkers have always ruled. They will continue to rule. The smart thing is to join them."

Part II

Using All of Your Mind

CHAPTER 4

The Gatekeeper

Who Wins, the Girl Next Door or the Prom Queen?

I like Katie Couric. Although she became the *CBS Evening News* anchor, what got her to that fifteen-million-dollar-a-year job was the personality she displayed on NBC's *Today* show.

She interviewed me a few times on the *Today* show, and she's every bit as cordial and charming in person as she appears on TV. Ms. Couric possesses a formidable combination of intellect, glamour, communicating presence, and girl-next-door congeniality. She is First-Brain-friendly. And that was an essential quality when Katie took over at the *Today* show in the early nineties.

Previously, Executive Producer Dick Ebersol had made a big mistake in trying to shore up slumping ratings. To replace Jane Pauley he moved the attractive Deborah Norville from reading news on *News at Sunrise* to the cohost slot on *Today*. Norville's sleek blond luster is justly matched by her intelligence and journalistic credibility. But she lacked warmth—she was to many like a distant prom queen.

The *Today* show ratings dropped from 4.4 and a 21 share to 3.8 and an 18 share—a shocking 14-percent decline. Heads rolled at NBC, since those lost ratings meant a slump of around twenty-five million dollars a year in ad revenue.

And then NBC finally saw the light, or stumbled into it, with Katie Couric. As Norville's temporary replacement during her pregnancy

Katie Couric (PETER KRAMER/GETTY IMAGES)

leave, Couric caught on with the public and the *Today* show ratings began climbing again. Why?

USA Today called Couric "the people's choice." She has a fresh, irreverent manner that connects. Bryant Gumbel said, "I can see most people relating to her almost like a little sister." And Couric, who peppers her conversations and interviews with humor, says of herself, "I didn't think I had the right stuff. I didn't think I was glamorous enough and that is probably still true." ABC's George Watson says that she has that "girl-next-door quality."

What was it about Katie Couric that made her worth twenty-five million dollars annually to NBC's bottom line? What did Katie Couric have that Deborah Norville didn't?

In a word, warmth. An open smile with just a touch of wry wit behind it. An honest sense of humor. A delightful sparkle. A bit of girl-next-doorishness. Katie Couric is a natural New Communicator.

Compared to all that, the best Deborah Norville had to offer was not bad—a sexy brand of competence and the cool, unapproachable beauty of a prom queen. But NBC seriously miscalculated in thinking the average viewer—male or female—would prefer to wake up and have breakfast with the prom queen rather than the girl next door.

If you want to wake up to someone who has energy, enthusiasm, and intellect, Katie's hard to beat. As Deborah Norville could tell her, glamour is not the key ingredient. Beauty and competence are not enough. They help, but to communicate effectively, we must make a personal connection.

Making Friends with the Gatekeeper

It should be obvious by now that effective communication is a lot more than simply transferring information from me to you, or vice versa. There is a gate between us through which communication must pass. The gate is tended by a Gatekeeper, standing guard before the House of the Intellect. The Gatekeeper's name is *First Brain.*

Will the Gatekeeper open or close the gate of communication? Will our message get through, or will it be blocked?

Whenever we communicate, our listener's Gatekeeper is right there on guard, figuratively asking, "Friend or foe?" The Gatekeeper has complete power to grant or deny access to our listener's higher analytic and decision-making processes. A New Communicator is a person who knows how to befriend the Gatekeeper, who knows how to become "First-Brain friendly," so that his or her message can get through effectively and persuasively.

FIRST-BRAIN POWER

Contrary to what you've probably been taught, effective communication is only partly concerned with our intellectual human brain, what I call the "New Brain." Before we can communicate effectively with our listener's New Brain, we must consider the hidden and generally unrecognized part of ourselves that I call the "First Brain." Though it is hidden from our consciousness, it is real, it is physical, and it is extremely powerful.

If the CBS brass had understood how the First Brain works, Dan Rather would have been out of there years earlier, and their third-rated evening news show would probably have been a first-rated show, hosted by Ted Koppel—or perhaps Jane Pauley.

If Michael Dukakis had understood how the First Brain works, he might have gone to the White House.

If Lee Raymond had understood how the First Brain works, he might have reversed the public, press, and political perceptions of Exxon. Instead of looking like the epitome of corporate evil, Exxon might have gained a reputation as a company that shoulders its responsibilities and fixes its mistakes.

Just a few pages from now, you will know what all of these people failed to understand. You will know how the First Brain works. And you'll know how to succeed where some of the brightest minds in business, politics, and the media have failed.

THE FIRST BRAIN REVEALED

You may be surprised to learn that your brain is not really one brain but several. You've probably heard about the differences between left-brain thinking and right-brain thinking, but that's not what we're talking about here. The truth is that many people emphasize only the left-brain/right-brain distinction (see box: "A Brain Myth"). Though there are differences between them, the left brain and right brain are actually just two halves of the highly developed cerebral cortex—what I call the "New Brain."

But there's a more important brain to be aware of, and knowing how this brain works can profoundly affect the way you communicate with others. This brain is a much more forceful and fundamental part of you than either the left or right brain. I call it the "First Brain."

The First Brain is the nonreasoning, nonrational part of our brain. Simply put, it is the seat of human emotion, composed of the brain stem and the limbic system. It's the most primitive part of the brain, consisting of components that existed between two hundred million and five hundred million years ago.

The New Brain is the cerebral cortex—that large, intricately folded, hemispherical mass that surrounds the more basic First Brain. The New Brain is the seat of conscious thought, memory, language, creativity, and decision making. I call it the New Brain because it is so recent compared with the First Brain, a mere three or four million years old.

When people communicate by the spoken word, they almost invariably aim their message at the New Brain and completely overlook the First Brain. That's why even such competent, intelligent people as Dan Rather, Lee Raymond, Deborah Norville, Bill Walsh, Jeanine Pirro, Michael Chertoff, and Mark McGwire fail to effectively get their message across to their audiences.

This is not to say that the New Brain is unimportant. On the contrary, our goal is to get our message across to the New Brain because that's the decision-making part of our mind. *But to reach the New Brain, our message must first pass through the First Brain, the emotional part of the*

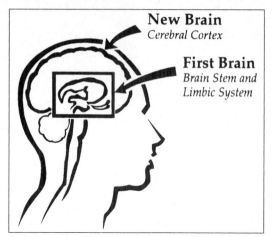

For a more detailed look at the First Brain, see Endnotes:
"The Brain within a Brain."[1]

brain. If we leave the First Brain out of the equation, our message will be distorted or diminished—or it may not get through at all.

The reason the First Brain is so important to effective communication is precisely because it is the seat of emotion and emotional response. It is clear that the most important language in effective communicating is almost an unspoken language, *the language of trust.* In Chapter 1 we discovered that in order to communicate effectively, we must make *emotional contact* with the listener. In Chapter 2, we learned *that people buy on emotion and justify with fact.* In Chapter 3, we learned that in the spoken medium, we must be *believed* in order to have impact, and that believability is overwhelmingly determined at *a preconscious* level.

Everything we've talked about in the first three chapters—emotional contact, emotional impact, believability, and trust—takes place in the preconscious realm of the First Brain. Though the goal of effective communication is to get our message across to the cerebral, rational processes of the New Brain, we can't do this without getting through to the First Brain first. It's the listener's First Brain that makes the decision whether or not to trust and believe the speaker. It's the First Brain that decides whether a person represents comfort and nurture—or anxiety and menace.

A BRAIN MYTH

"Everybody knows" that all human thought is neatly divided between the two hemispheres of our brain—our left and right brains. The linear thought processes of language, logic, and mathematics occur in the left brain. The conceptual thought processes of art, music, creativity, and inspiration occur on the right.

The problem with what "everybody knows" is that much of it just ain't so.

Though left-brain/right-brain lateralization is a well-established fact, documented by the "brain-mapping" research of Nobel Prize–winner Roger Sperry, most people have a grossly distorted and oversimplified view of what this really means. The left and right brains are often misconstrued to be totally separate systems. Though separated from each other by a deep vertical cleft, the left and right hemispheres of the brain are kept in constant communication and coordination via the corpus callosum—a thick, cablelike structure containing thousands of information channels.

Supposed left-brain functions such as language actually involve both hemispheres. Researchers have found that the language in a good story or novel tends to excite as much or more brain activity in the right hemisphere as in the left. Researchers have also found that if the "speech centers" in the left brain are injured, the right brain is frequently able to take over some of the language functions of the left brain.

While there are definite differences between the functions of the left brain and the right brain, these distinctions pale into insignificance compared with the all-important contrast between the New Brain and the First Brain. The task of a New Communicator is not just to reach the right brain or the left brain, the two halves of the New Brain. The New Communicator's real task is to reach the First Brain.

The key to understanding the First Brain is realizing that its essential purpose is survival. The two basic parts of the First Brain are sometimes called the reptilian and mammalian brains, for that is almost all that those creatures have. And for them, the purpose of the First Brain is primary and essential—they must immediately feel and react to danger. For that is what the First Brain basically does. It quickly analyzes all incoming data in light of the question "Is this situation safe?"

Now we human beings have a highly specialized, complex, sophisticated, and astounding New Brain that *thinks*. But, surprisingly enough, the role of our First Brain remains essentially the same as it always was.

First Brain and New Brain Compared

First Brain

♥ Instinctual and Primitive
♥ 300 to 500 million years old
♥ Emotional
♥ Preconscious/Unconscious
♥ Source of instinctive survival responses: hunger, thirst, danger, sex, and parental care
♥ Common to many animals

New Brain

♦ Intellectual and Advanced
♦ 3 to 4 million years old
♦ Rational
♦ Conscious
♦ Source of thought, memory, language, creativity, planning, and decision making
♦ Uniquely human

New Brain:
The folds of the cerebrum consist of a very thin (⅛-inch thick) layer of brain cells called the Cerebral Cortex. All conscious thought takes place within this thin layer of brain cells.

First Brain:

Limbic System, the emotional center

Brain Stem, providing immediate instinctual response

Even in an ordinary, civilized, social conversation between two human beings in the twenty-first century, our First Brains are still only interested in one question: "Is it safe?"

If you want to get your message across, you must reach and connect with the First Brain. You must persuade your listener's First Brain that you are trustworthy, that you are likable, that you represent warmth, comfort, and safety.

HOW THE FIRST BRAIN WORKS

Now at this point you may be thinking, "All this stuff about the brain—isn't that too complicated for me to understand?" Sure, the human brain is a very complex organ, and we are only beginning to fathom it. But there have been important and exciting new discoveries in brain research in recent years. And applying these exciting revelations of what we *do* know to the communications process is really very simple to explain and understand. *Most important of all, the First Brain concept is a powerful and transforming new truth.* Isn't it worth understanding a few simple facts about our complex human brain in order to gain the power to achieve what you want in life?

The profound role of the First Brain in the communications process has been virtually ignored by communications experts and theorists until now. With the unveiling of the First-Brain concept, we suddenly have more at our disposal than a grab bag of "public speaking" techniques. We now have *knowledge*—an understanding of why certain behaviors work and others don't. And that knowledge has the power to make us more effective and persuasive every time we speak.

Now we know that all the hundreds of sights and sounds we give off as communicators—all the visual and auditory cues we project—must first pass through the figurative switching station of the listener's First Brain. This emotion-powered switching station inside our listener's head determines if we are believable, likable, and worth listening to. Everything we say—all the stimuli we communicate—is filtered and modified by the listener's First Brain before it is sent on to his or her New Brain—the cerebral cortex—to be analyzed and acted upon.

> Much evidence now indicates that the limbic area [First Brain] is the main switch in determining what sensory inputs will go to the neocortex and what decisions will be accepted *from* it . . .
>
> —Leslie A. Hart
>
> from *How the Brain Works*

If we are energetic, enthusiastic, and believable, our words will actually be given more impact and energy by the listener's First Brain before they are switched to the New Brain. But if we appear boring, anxious, or insincere, our words may not even reach their destination. Instead, our message will be discolored or even tuned out at the switching station by our lack of believability. If we lack believability, we risk failure in all the areas of our lives that really matter to us.

To be persuasive and successful, we must be believed, and belief is overwhelmingly determined by the preconscious mechanism of the First Brain.

FIRST-BRAIN-FRIENDLY

How, then, do we make friends with the Gatekeeper—the First Brain—so that our message can get through the gate? How do we become "First-Brain-friendly?"

By being natural. By learning to use energy, enthusiasm, motion, expression—all the multichannel, nonverbal cues that enable us to make emotional contact with the listener. By becoming freer, less inhibited, more naturally ourselves.

In his outstanding book *Blink: The Power of Thinking Without Thinking,* Malcolm Gladwell underscores the awesome power of the First Brain in our communicating experiences. He uses a different term for the First Brain, calling it the "adaptive unconscious," but the meaning is the same. Drawing upon evidence from cognitive research, Gladwell describes a principle of automated and unconscious perception that he calls "thin-slicing." He writes:

> "Thin-slicing" refers to the ability of our unconscious to find patterns in situations and behavior based on very narrow slices of experience. . . . Thin-slicing is part of what makes the unconscious

so dazzling. But it's also what we find most problematic about rapid cognition. How is it possible to gather the necessary information for a sophisticated judgment in such a short time? . . . When we leap to a decision or have a hunch, our unconscious is . . . sifting through the situation in front of us, throwing out all that is irrelevant while we zero in on what really matters. And the truth is that our unconscious is really good at this, to the point where thin-slicing often delivers a better answer than more deliberate and exhaustive ways of thinking.[2]

Gladwell describes a controlled scientific experiment that demonstrates the power of thin-slicing to form amazingly accurate judgments in as little as two seconds. In the experiment, psychologist Nalini Ambady showed a group of students three ten-second video clips without sound. Each video clip showed a teacher conducting a class. The students rated each teacher's effectiveness based solely on that silent ten-second snippet of video.

Next, Ambady cut the silent video clips in half, to five seconds, and showed them to a new group of students. The students rated each teacher's effectiveness—and the ratings were absolutely consistent with the ratings of the ten-second clips.

Ambady repeated the experiment with silent video clips that were only *two seconds* in length. Even though the student reviewers could do nothing more than make a snap judgment, their ratings were remarkably consistent with the ratings based on five- and ten-second video clips.

Finally, Ambady compared the two-second snap judgments against written evaluations of the same teachers—evaluations made by classroom students after a *full semester* of instruction by those teachers. The two-second snap judgments were remarkably consistent with the semester evaluations! "That's the power of the adaptive unconscious," Gladwell concludes.[3]

Or, as I would put it, that's the power of the First Brain.

We all engage in thin-slicing. We all make two-second snap judgments about people and situations—and those snap judgments are remarkably accurate, even though they are intuitive rather than rational and logical.

Even more important is the fact that people are constantly thin-slicing us! They are reaching snap judgments, forming opinions, and making decisions about us in as little as two seconds. Does this knowledge frighten you? Don't let it. Instead, let this knowledge motivate and empower you to become a First-Brain-friendly communicator. Use this knowledge to magnify your effectiveness as a speaker.

When you give a presentation, consider how your audience will view you—especially in the first two seconds of your presentation. Remember, people will form opinions and make decisions about you and your message in the blink of an eye. Make sure they don't tune you out or put up barriers. Be likable, expressive, energetic, and enthusiastic. Be natural.

Reach out and grab them by the First Brain from the very first word—then don't let go! Hook them, fascinate them, and engage them—and you *will* persuade them.

New Communicators succeed where Old Communicators fail because—either intuitively or intentionally—New Communicators have learned to be First-Brain-friendly. They know how to befriend the Gatekeeper within their listeners—and that's the knowledge they need to persuade others and to achieve their own goals. The Gatekeeper—the First Brain, the adaptive unconscious—can either lock and bolt the door and block your message, or it can fling the door wide to receive your message.

It all depends on you.

In the rest of this book we'll learn some powerful behavioral habits and techniques you can use to become First-Brain-friendly—plus you'll learn how to control your own First Brain to overcome the fear of public speaking.

From now on, think First Brain.

CHAPTER 5

Getting to Trust

The next time you see an Orlando Magic basketball game, think "talk." The Magic organization exists today because of one man's skills as a talker. His name is Pat Williams, and he's the senior vice president of the Orlando Magic.

"Over the years," Pat told me, "I've given thousands of speeches. To this day, I speak at least a hundred and fifty times a year. I remember Miss Barbara Bullard's English class. She made us give an entire speech from a single three-by-five card—and I would put an entire word-for-word script in tiny lettering on that card! Needless to say, I was the worst public speaker in the ninth grade. If you'd told me I would spend my adult life giving speeches, I would have refused to grow up!

"The Orlando Magic exists today because of thousands and thousands of hours of talk. The idea for the team was born while I was in Orlando for a speaking engagement. I was general manager of the Philadelphia 76ers at the time, and I was speaking at the First Presbyterian Church in Orlando. Afterwards, one of the pastors, John Tolson, and a local businessman, Jimmy Hewitt, drove me to the airport. During the ride, I asked, 'Do you think pro basketball would fly in Florida?' They said, 'Absolutely.' I said, 'Where? Miami or Tampa?' They said, 'Neither! The future is in Orlando!'

"Long story short, I was captivated by the idea of starting an NBA franchise right next door to Walt Disney World. So I started building the dream with Jimmy Hewitt and some other Orlando businesspeople.

I began by taking a huge career risk: I quit my job with the 76ers and moved my family to Orlando. There was no guarantee Orlando would get a team. In fact, with Miami, Tampa, Minnesota, Toronto, Charlotte, and Anaheim all seeking an expansion team, the odds were against us.

"Job One was building trust. I had to convince the media and the citizens of Orlando that we were going to build a team to be proud of. I had to convince the town fathers to build an arena and grant us a whole host of favors to make it possible for the team to do business.

"Starting an expansion team from scratch is a classic chicken-egg problem. The NBA doesn't want to award a franchise until they know that the community is going to buy tons of season tickets—and fans won't buy season tickets until there's a franchise. So I was constantly going around to the Kiwanis and Rotary clubs, various civic groups, the Chamber of Commerce, and so forth, talking up the Magic and selling season tickets for a team that might never exist. I was determined to gain the trust of a skeptical community.

"I was in a nonstop selling mode. I'd speak at a men's breakfast, a community luncheon, a press conference, a sports dinner, then on the way home, I'd stop at the health food store and make my pitch to customers while in the checkout line.

"I had to pull off an occasional stunt to get attention. At one press conference, I started disrobing as I talked. I removed my coat and tie, and as I started unbuttoning my shirt, I could see the audience was getting nervous. I pulled off my shirt and revealed a printed T-shirt that read: 'Orlando—On the Way to the NBA!' That got attention.

"At another press conference, I listed all the great things Orlando had to offer an NBA franchise. I concluded by mentioning a nearby city that was also competing for a franchise: 'And we all know the problems Miami has.' That comment was picked up and magnified by the media. The following day, the *Miami Herald* ran the headline 'Orlando's Williams Blasts Miami.' Whoa! That set off the first Miami-Orlando 'grapefruit war'—a friendly but intense rivalry that continues to this day.

"I made trips to New York and personally lobbied NBA commissioner David Stern. I took that short trip over to the Magic Kingdom and met with Disney's then CEO Michael Eisner about a possible Disney-Magic partnership. In order to get funding, I made the pitch to potential investors.

"It was talking that brought the fan base together, talking that brought the community on board, talking that convinced the NBA to grant the franchise, talking that put together the millions needed to build an arena and a sports organization. In order to build a dream as big and expensive as an NBA team, you need to build excitement and trust—and that takes communication.

"I'm sure Miss Barbara Bullard would hardly believe how far one of her old students has come as a talker. I know I showed exactly zero promise when I was in her ninth grade class. But I'm here to tell you that if you want to accomplish something big, if you want to attract people to your cause and build support for your efforts, you've got to become a communicator."

The Language of Trust

In our communication with others, trust and believability are inter-changeable. You can't believe a person unless you trust that person. You can't trust that person unless you can believe what they say.

To communicate persuasively and effectively, you must win the trust of your listeners. And to win their trust, you must be believable. How do you do it?

Belief is a First-Brain function. Belief is acceptance on faith. Some people will believe you on first impression. Most need at least a little convincing. They need to see you, hear you, and interact with you before they can invest their trust and belief in you. Either way, belief is based on emotion. It bypasses the intellect. It comes from the nuances of behavior, not from facts or logic. It is perceived and felt rather than analyzed.

The First Brain houses the labyrinth of our emotional makeup—and I do not use the word *labyrinth* as a mere metaphor. Look at the picture of the limbic system, a major component of the First Brain

(Endnotes, Chapter 4), and you can see that it is physically shaped like a labyrinth, intricate and convoluted. The hidden urges and needs that drive human behavior, and which often seem so murky and mysterious to our logical minds, arise from the depths of the First Brain.

The First Brain does not understand words. It speaks an altogether different language: the language of behavior. Whereas our New Brain (the cerebral cortex) spends most of its time sifting words, symbols, concepts, and data, the First Brain hunts for meaning in thousands of nuances of human behavior that the New Brain never even registers. Does the voice quaver—or project a sense of authority? Do the hands fidget nervously—or gesture forcefully? Do the eyes flicker hesitantly— or smile unflinchingly? Is the posture diffident—or confident?

That's the language of the First Brain, the language of trust. It's a language that is learned very early in life.

THE COMMUNICATING WISDOM OF CHILDREN

Watch a child during the first six months of life. Study the child closely—the wide eyes that take in every movement, that quick glance at every sound. Observe how the child responds to a gentle touch, a murmured reassurance, a smile—especially a smile! That child has no language, no preconceptions, no categories with which to make sense of his or her world.

Very little of what a baby perceives is imprinted on his or her New Brain. Most of the sights and sounds of a baby's world are traced in the neurons (brain cells) of the First Brain. You can communicate with a baby, but not with words. To communicate with a baby, you use facial expression, energy, sound, touch, and motion. The baby responds with the same set of nonverbal cues. That's the language of First-Brain communication.

The First Brain is being imprinted even before birth, while the baby is still in the womb. The First Brain experiences the warmth and comfort of the womb. It receives the sounds of the mother's steadily pulsing heart, her gentle respiration, her musical laughter, her complaints, her sighs. The First Brain of an unborn child is learning at a primitive level about contentment, warmth, safety, and trust. Soon, the child will learn about discomfort, the cold sensation of a draft on skin, the strange sights and noises of life outside the womb.

During a layover at Kennedy International Airport in New York, I struck up a conversation with a young woman who was traveling with two children, a four-year-old boy and a little girl who was just a babe in arms.

"Beautiful baby," I said. "She must be about six months old."

The mother smiled. "Yes," she replied proudly. "This is Susie." Susie cooed contentedly. "And this is Timmy," she said, nodding to the boy. Timmy shied away. Something in his First Brain told him to be wary of strangers.

"Tell me," I said, "who was the first person Susie recognized beside yourself?"

"Well," she said, "Susie made goo-goo sounds at Timmy when she was about a week old. I think she recognized him as early as that."

"When did she recognize her dad?"

"She smiled at him when she was about a month old. She's only begun recognizing friends and relatives in the last couple of months. And she doesn't warm up to strangers at all." Susie is a typical baby. Her First Brain is functioning right on cue. In the first few weeks of her life, she was already using her First-Brain programming, learning whom to trust and why.

Susie knows she can trust Mother (her primary caregiver); she can trust another Little Person (her four-year-old brother, Timmy); and, in time, she can even trust Daddy and friends of the family. She knows that a smile means attention and fun, and that a soothing touch means nurture and warmth. Over the next year she may also learn that a person who doesn't smile is likely to lack warmth, and may act unpleasantly.

The point is that most of the learning we experience in the first few weeks and months of life is First-Brain learning. It is our First Brain, not our New Brain, that receives most of the imprinting in those early stages of life. Those deeply etched imprints stay with us forever. One of those imprints is a program for determining whom we trust, and why. We learn early that people who smile and radiate warmth and composure are safer than those who don't. These qualities attracted and reassured us when we were small and helpless, and these same qualities are no less important to us now that we are grown.

To communicate effectively, we must relearn the language of trust, the language of emotional contact . . .

The language of the First Brain.

GROKKING AND BEING GROKKED

Did you ever interview someone for a position in your company and immediately *know* they were the person for the job? But you didn't know why. Did you ever hear a radio sportscaster or talk show host and immediately turn him off because he turned you off? But you didn't know why. Did you ever catch the eye of another person and just know you have fallen completely and instantly in love? But you didn't know why.

Then you know what it means to *grok*.

If you're a Robert Heinlein fan, you know that the word *grok* comes from his novel *Stranger in a Strange Land*. Heinlein's protagonist, Valentine Michael Smith, had the ability to grok, to instantly grasp the inner reality of people and situations. Smith, of course, was an alien, a "man from Mars," so his grokking is a science-fictional ability that doesn't exist in the real world. After all, it's logically impossible to immediately know and understand another person almost as soon as you meet them, isn't it?

Or is it?

The fact is, we grok people all the time—and we are continually being grokked. Of course, none of us are aliens, so we can't grok as fully and deeply as Valentine Michael Smith. But we are better grokkers than we realize.

In every new situation, your First Brain receives thousands of cues that are registered at the preconscious level. You form impressions of people and situations, and you call it "intuition." Your impressions are colored with emotion. The more you learn to plug into and trust your ability to grok people and intuit situations, the more useful this ability becomes.

Our Western cultural tendency is to approach communication as if it were all a matter of rational New Brain content, facts, arguments, and logic. In fact, an equal or greater part of all human communication consists of First-Brain intuition. This amazing human ability to glimpse a profound truth in an instant of time is important to all of our relationships, from business relationships to matters of the heart.

A glimpse of the truth. I met Bev Moore when I was an undergrad at Yale. I was dating a girl in Bev's dorm at Smith College at the time. The first moment I laid eyes on Bev, I fell for her. She had sparkle and spunk and an athletic vitality packed into a slight frame—not to mention her silky blond hair, blue eyes, and an upturned nose. We saw a lot of movies together, skied together on weekends, and laughed a lot. I was in love, and so was she.

One weekend, after we had been dating for about eight months, Bev took the train from Northampton to New Haven to visit me. It was a gloomy weekend with a cold, gray, threatening sky.

On Saturday we went to the football game at the Yale Bowl. Yale lost in an upset. We were invited to a party that night, but we declined and took in a movie instead. I don't remember what movie, but I do recall that it was depressing.

Sunday was no better. There was no fight, no argument. Just . . . distance. Bev was moody, and she became more withdrawn as the weekend progressed. I asked her what was wrong. She couldn't say. Defensively and selfishly, I became distant and uncaring in response.

As I took her to the train station to see her off, the skies fulfilled their gloomy promise, dumping a cold rain on us to match the chill we both felt inside. Standing by the train, we kissed—a brief and perfunctory kiss. I was aching inside.

"Good-bye, Bev," I said, searching her eyes. I could read nothing there.

"Good-bye, Bert," she said, stepping onto the train. She was nearly the last passenger to board, and the train began moving just seconds after I lost sight of her.

I stood and watched to see if I could catch another glimpse of her. I didn't want to lose her, but there was a wall between us that I didn't understand. *She doesn't care,* I thought. *Okay, I don't care either.*

Then I saw her, framed in one of the parlor car windows. She didn't see me. It was only a glimpse as the train moved away—no more than a second. But what I saw pierced me like an arrow. Her face fell into her hands and her shoulders trembled. She was crying!

I saw our whole relationship in that brief glimpse. I knew she still cared. Suddenly, I was more in love than ever. I could hardly wait for her to get back to Smith so we could talk on the phone. I experienced that whole kaleidoscope of emotions in a fraction of a second.

That's how the First Brain works. It understands at a preconscious, nonverbal level. It transforms a gesture, a glance, an inflection into insight, understanding, and emotion. It sees everything in an instant.

"First-Brain-Friendly" Wins

To be an effective communicator, you must become "First-Brain-friendly"—open, unaffected, spontaneous, and natural. A First-Brain-friendly communicator is confident and at ease, not stiff or nervous. When we are relaxed and confident, we put our listener's First Brain at ease so that he or she can trust us and believe our message.

A person who is First-Brain-friendly is likable—and likability is the shortest path to believability and trust. Pollster George Gallup proved the importance of likability. He conducted a series of political polls that revealed a phenomenon he called the "Personality Factor." The results can be seen most dramatically in his polling for presidential elections.

One of the most vivid examples of the Personality Factor is the Gallup Poll conducted during the 1984 presidential election. In September 1984, two months before the election, Gallup measured candidates Ronald Reagan and Walter Mondale for three factors: issues, party affiliation, and likability. To scientifically quantify the likability factor, he used the Staples Scalometer, a 5-point variable where people state their emotional response to a candidate.

Let's look at the first two factors, issues and party affiliation. On issues, Gallup found that Reagan and Mondale were neck and neck in the polls—42 percent to 42 percent. But on party affiliation, Mondale had a clear edge because of Democrat-registered voters: Mondale's 42 percent to Reagan's 28 percent.

On the scale of likability, there was a very different story. Using the Staples Scalometer, Gallup found that on a feeling level, the level of trust and likability, Reagan had a clear advantage over Mondale. The poll showed that 42 percent of those questioned found Reagan likable versus 26 percent for Mondale—a 16-point advantage for Reagan.

If all three measurements were equal in importance, the 1984 election would have been a photo finish, with Mondale edging out Reagan by a mere 2 percent. But that's not the way it went down—*because these three measurements are not equal in importance*. The final election tally mirrors almost exactly the likability factor of the poll two months earlier: 59 percent for Reagan versus Mondale's 41 percent—an 18-point margin for Reagan.

Sure, we pride ourselves on our rational assessment of the issues facing our nation, and some of us even pride ourselves on our party loyalty. But when the chips are down, it's likability that wins.

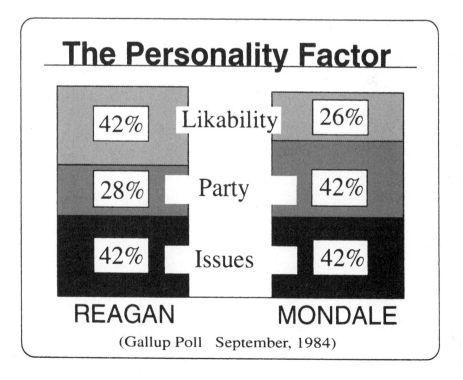

The Personality Factor

	REAGAN		MONDALE
Likability	42%		26%
Party	28%		42%
Issues	42%		42%

(Gallup Poll   September, 1984)

George Gallup has conducted the Personality Factor poll prior to every presidential election since Nixon-Kennedy in 1960, the beginning of the television age of politics. In all that time, one factor has always been a consistent prognosticator of the final election results: the likability factor.

The likability factor dominates in politics. It dominates in business. And it dominates in our day-to-day lives. Likability is the key to trust and believability.

The Great Communicator

Some say Ronald Reagan was the Great Communicator. Others say Bill Clinton. I would nominate another candidate. You probably haven't heard his name before—but someday you may hear a lot about him. His name: Nido Qubein.

Nido is a remarkable businessman, entrepreneur, visionary, author, speaker, chairman of many boards and companies, and the president of High Point University in North Carolina. If he wanted to go into politics, I have no doubt he could give any career politician a run for his money.

He arrived in the United States from Lebanon with fifty dollars in his pocket. He taught himself English and became a master and teacher of the art of communication. He is a consummate professional who lives the principles he teaches. I've personally seen him put together a powerful, persuasive talk in a matter of minutes—and when he delivered his talk, he had the audience in the palm of his hand.

Nido Qubein uses his considerable communicating skills to promote the university. In his first eighteen months as president of High Point University, he raised a hundred million dollars in donations, oversaw the completion and renovation of ten buildings, and increased enrollment dramatically. Moreover, faculty and staff give him the credit for a huge upswing in motivation and morale at the university.

I spent a day on the campus with Nido and twenty friends and associates from the Speakers Roundtable. Though we are all successful people in our own spheres of influence, we were in awe of what Nido

Nido Qubein

had accomplished in a year and a half. More important, we were amazed at the warm and friendly relationships he had with students, faculty, and staff.

Psychologist and speaker Terry Paulson, in his LeaderLine blog (http://terrypaulson.typepad.com/leaderline/), made an observation that says a lot about Nido's personality and the way he builds trust with his students: "Nido Qubein's office doesn't have a closed door. Instead it has a bubble gum machine right outside. Students are invited to come by and talk. He feels that by rewarding students who have the confidence to come talk to him with gum, he's sending an important message. It isn't just what you know and learn that counts in life; you have to have the confidence to network and share your concerns and perspectives with others."[1]

Nido Qubein inspires First-Brain trust in everyone he talks to. He's authentic, sincere, and believable. When he accepted the challenge of presiding over the transformation at High Point University, he came in with a bold vision. He couldn't do the job of raising money, building new structures, and changing the culture of an academic institution all by himself. He needed to get people to trust him, buy into his vision, and see it through to completion.

And that's exactly what he did. He built trust and confidence through his speaking ability, his open door policy, and his accessibility. When I was with him on the campus, he was continually being greeted, high-fived, and hugged wherever he went.

I asked a member of his staff, a young man named Chris, how Nido was to work for. "Great," Chris said. "He sets high goals and standards, but he's fair and he appreciates the people who work with him. He pays attention to every detail, and when things are done well, he's very generous with compliments."

Nido himself shared the secret of his ability to create believability and trust through communication. "You have to be real," he said. "You have to communicate who you are. Be natural. Let the real you come through! When people see that you are comfortable with who you are, they trust you."

Reading Speeches, Losing Audiences

Once, during a layover at Chicago's O'Hare airport, I was making phone calls in the Red Carpet Club, waiting for my flight. I noticed a couple of businessmen at a nearby table working on a sales presentation. They had their jackets off, their sleeves rolled up, and they were poring over a mountain of slides. Next to Mount PowerPoint was another mountain made of paper. It was the script for their presentation, and it had to be every bit of twenty or thirty pages long, single-spaced.

I thought, *Woe betide the listeners doomed to endure this slide marathon!* Imagine the boredom, the mass tune-out, the glazed stares! Pity those poor, tortured First Brains in the audience, silently crying out for sustenance and relief! They will drown in data while thirsting for knowledge.

Don't do that to your listeners. And don't do it to yourself.

I've seen it so many times. One of the most glaring examples occurred when I was keynote speaker at a meeting of the National Fire Sprinkler Association, with over a hundred owners and managers of fire sprinkler manufacturing and distributing companies gathered at a major downtown hotel.

There were several speakers ahead of me, most speaking on fairly technical subjects—manufacturing processes, the financial climate, and government regulations. The first speaker had lots of detailed information, lots of handouts, and an annoyingly whiny voice. With all those handouts in their grasp, everybody was too busy reading to listen to the speaker. Which was just as well.

We could be in for a long day, I thought to myself. And unfortunately for me, I was the third and final speaker scheduled for the morning.

The next speaker had slides. Lots of slides. Almost as many as those guys in the Red Carpet Club at O'Hare. Some people in the audience watched those PowerPoints as if hypnotized. Some tried to read newspapers by the light from the screen. The speaker read his speech in a phlegmatic drone. At the end, there was no applause, just a mass sigh of relief.

The energy in that room was so low that I hesitated to do my normal opening, which almost always works. I deliberately start a presentation in the worst possible way. I lay a stack of pages (supposedly the text of my speech) on the lectern and start reading. Eyes glued to the page. Flat monotone voice. No gestures. In other words, just like my two predecessors on that podium.

I decided to go with it anyway. After I was introduced, I stepped up to the lectern and proceeded to do everything I could to sabotage my own likability and drive the energy of the audience into the ground. It worked beautifully. In seconds, the boredom in that room was so thick you'd have to cut it with a chainsaw.

I glanced up a couple of times as I droned on—not to make eye contact with my listeners, but just to make sure that they were still tuned out. It was perfect. I saw people yawning, gazing blankly, reading newspapers, checking watches.

Then, about a minute into my speech, I raised my voice, picked up my "notes," tossed them behind me, and stepped out from behind the lectern. A ripple of surprise and a murmur of suspense went through the audience. I could see it in their faces: *What is this guy up to?* I now had their undivided attention.

"How many of you completely tuned out while I was talking from that lectern?" No hands. "Oh, come on! Be honest! I just got through boring you to tears! Admit it! How many of you tuned me out completely in the first five seconds of my so-called speech?" Grins now— and a massive show of hands.

From that point on we were off and running. The energy level of the audience soared. Those poor suffering souls were ecstatic! Somebody finally cared enough to communicate with them! They were starving for real human contact!

People don't want facts and figures. They want someone to listen to. Someone to *like*.

A Memory Test

Whenever I open a speech that way, I use real content, not nonsense. I start by talking about how we, as communicators at all levels, need to make emotional contact with our listeners and keep them involved, while at that very time I'm doing my best to turn my listeners off! In fact, to underscore my message, I always give some simple facts and figures that support my content.

Then, after I move out from behind the lectern, make the transition, begin to contact the people, with the energy level leaping, I ask, "Does anyone remember those four points I made? . . . Two of the points? . . . One? Oh, come on! Somebody here must remember at least one out of four!"

I can usually find one or two volunteers who can remember one of my points, maybe two. Everyone else draws a complete blank. They got absolutely none of the facts I read to them only a couple of minutes before! But when I bring the energy up, retention zooms! If you want your message to be memorable and persuasive, it's not enough to buttress it with facts and figures. You must reach the First Brain. You must use communicating behavior that produces belief and trust.

The wrong behavior turns people off. They won't hear you. They won't remember you. They won't even like you. They certainly won't be persuaded by anything you say. The First Brain has shut the doors and barred the gates—and you're left out in the cold.

Let me tell you a story to prove the point.

At 6 feet 7 inches, Tom Troja is a big dude (he gave me permission to share this story, by the way). Some years back, he headed up our New York office. One fall, after a great sales year, Tom flew to San Francisco for the fall quarterly review. He was stoked, absolutely brimming with energy, as he made his presentation. He was doing an outstanding job in New York, and he knew it.

As he unveiled the sales quotas he'd projected for October, November, and December, someone pointed to the December quota. It was quite a bit lower than the other months' quotas. Several people in the room started to quiz Tom about that December quota. "Where did that number come from?" "Why so pessimistic, Tom?" "What do you base that on?"

Tom became defensive and tried to justify the number. Suddenly he wasn't stoked anymore. In fact, his irritation was showing—big-time. He clearly felt he was being picked on because of one number on a chart.

And you know, he had a right to feel that way. Tom was a top producer and he was having a great year, but people were zeroing in on a little island of negativity in an ocean of good news. Tom was a competent, effective, likable guy—but at that moment, he wasn't so likable. His defensiveness and resentment at the very end of the presentation wiped out all the good vibes that had gone before.

Contrast Tom's presentation with that of Fred Verhey at the same meeting. Fred was our vice president of Training and Operations—and he was not having such a great year in the Speaker Services division. His division's revenues were well under projection for the quarter. In fact, his division's entire year had been pretty lackluster—and Fred knew it. We all knew it.

So what did Fred do? He came in and started his presentation like a game of *Jeopardy*. His presentation had its share of bad news—but Fred chose to have fun with it. The numbers were bad, the projections weren't much better—but the mood in the room was positive. Fred was smiling—and so was everyone else. Fred wasn't trying to spin the facts or slip bad news by us—we all recognized the bad news for what it was. But he was upbeat and enthusiastic about his prospects for improving those numbers. He wasn't going to let a bad quarter beat him down. He ended the presentation on a high note.

Tom Troja served up great numbers but undermined them with defensiveness. Fred Verhey served up lousy numbers but pulled it off with optimism and a positive attitude. What carried the day?

Likability. People who are likable win our trust and support.

Let's Take a Vote

A while back, I was invited by Radius Scientific to address a large gathering of neurologists at the Silverado Country Club in the heart of the Napa Valley. I was speaking on a subject familiar to you by now: "Communicating Is a Contact Sport." The group was interested in relating the link between communication and the human brain to their work. Much of the morning was devoted to talks about a new drug treatment for strokes, and most of the content revolved around technical minutiae—the effects of certain pharmacological agents on the hematology of the brain, and the like.

Once again I was about to go out in front of a low-energy audience. Should I use the turnaround routine again? Would it work again? The academic nature of the audience introduced a new variable into the equation. This group might be harder to turn than the previous low-energy audience.

But this group also presented an opportunity I'd never had before: IRIS.

IRIS is an audience interactive device. Each listener in the audience is given a remote keypad with which to instantly vote on questions or issues. Radius Scientific had brought in the IRIS system to get audience feedback. I couldn't resist the opportunity to perform a live experiment regarding emotional connection and likability.

I began with a boring, flat opening. I read my speech for a minute, then—still reading in my bone-dry monotone—I said, "I would like you all to use your IRIS device and answer the following question: At this moment, how open are you to the ideas of this presentation and this presenter? (1) Like very much; (2) Like somewhat; (3) Neutral; (4) Dislike; (5) Dislike very much."

The audience voted—and just as I expected, I bombed! I was a disaster! (See the chart below.)

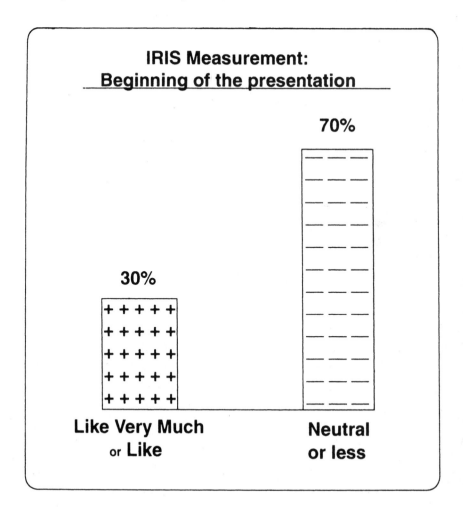

Then I shifted to my normal presentation mode, replete with energy, enthusiasm, eye contact, and a big warm smile. The mood shift in the room was palpable. For the rest of the hour I told them—and showed them—what it means to make emotional contact, to speak the nonverbal language of the First Brain.

Though no one was bored, I could tell there were pockets of resistance. A number of these cerebral, intellectually oriented men and women had a hard time accepting my assertion that human beings buy on emotion, not fact. It's hard when your lifelong focus has been on hard facts and cognitive data to suddenly adopt a new paradigm regarding the way our brains process communication.

Over time, the resistance melted. We had fun together. After a while, I could see it in their eyes and their smiles: I had won them over. I had gained their trust. I had persuaded them of the need to make an emotional connection, to reach the First Brain.

Toward the end of the hour, I again asked for a vote. The result was immediate, as the chart on page 97 shows.

There was nearly a threefold increase in likability. Here is a precise measurement of communication effectiveness—the kind of scientific measurement that even our reasoning New Brains can understand.

And consider this: What kind of communication occurs in a group that is 70 percent neutral or disliking the speaker? Hardly any at all! But when 80 percent of the audience members like, trust, and believe in the speaker, the message will be believed and heard.

A Tremendous Communicator

Let me tell you about a man named Charlie "Tremendous" Jones.

His two passions are reading and speaking. He often says, "You are the same today as you'll be in five years except for two things: the people you meet and the books you read." Visit his home and you'll see an amazing collection of books, including nearly three hundred books on Lincoln, nearly a hundred books on George Washington, plus a vast

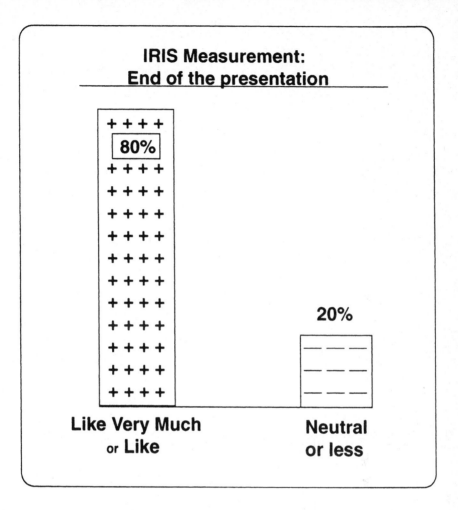

number of books by Oswald Chambers. Charlie is also the author of *Life Is Tremendous,* which has sold more than two million copies.

Where did he get the nickname "Tremendous"? He humbly explains, "I'm a man of limited vocabulary. After years of signing my letters 'Tremendous' and calling my friends 'Tremendous' and saying that life is 'Tremendous,' it stuck."

Charlie "Tremendous" Jones is one of the most likable and persuasive speakers I've ever heard. When he takes the podium, his personality lights up the room. A dapper dresser, Charlie always wears a trim dark suit and bow tie.

Charlie Jones

He makes everyone in the audience feel energized, empowered, and good about themselves. He's a hugger. He picks people out of the audience, compliments their smile, and gives them great big bear hugs. He has a special gift for making people laugh.

Whenever Charlie speaks, one thing comes through loud and clear: Charlie loves people and he loves to fire people up with enthusiasm! He's passionate about books, about living a positive and successful life, about traditional family values, and about his strong faith in God.

Has Charlie always been so infectiously positive and optimistic? Actually, no. He tells a story about how his mother abandoned the family when Charlie was just eleven, the oldest of five children. He grew up with a huge hole in his life where a mother's love should have been. Sometimes she'd come to visit, and Charlie hoped she'd come to stay—but soon she'd leave and young Charlie would be more embittered than before. Early in his life, he vowed that when he grew up and had children, his mother would never be allowed to see them. Charlie intended to have his revenge.

He grew up, married a young woman named Gloria (to whom he's still married today), and their first child was born, a little boy. Charlie's mother lived just a mile away, but he refused to let her see her grandson. Then, as Charlie tells it, "A truck driver introduced me to the love of God and His forgiveness. I realized immediately how wrong I was. I went to my mother and I had to ask her to forgive me for the resentment I'd carried all those years."

After that, Charlie maintained a relationship with his mother. He bought her a home, called her weekly, took her on a trip to Europe, and at the end of her life, gave the eulogy at her funeral. Charlie is a positive, inspiring author and speaker today because he made a decision to forgive and be forgiven.

When he tells that story, there's not a dry eye in the room. By being

vulnerable and open about his own hurts, he makes an emotional connection. He creates instant trust and believability. People trust Charlie
because he's absolutely genuine—the real deal.

Oh, and one more thing about Charlie. Back in the 1960s, he built
a hundred-million-dollar-a-year insurance business. He retired at age
thirty-seven so he could devote himself to speaking and writing. Charlie is a very rich man—but compared with his love for people, his love
for God, and his personal genuineness and integrity, the little matter of
his material wealth is a mere footnote.

Charlie seems to have an intuitive understanding that speaking is
not just a matter of dispensing words, but of making an emotional
connection. "Words are but tools," he once said. "The voice conveys
the meaning. The tone of the voice tells whether you are friendly or are
looking for a fight. The average person is more susceptible to the
change in tone in the voice than to any select set of words. It's not so
much what you say as how you say it."

That's the essence of this chapter: You've got to be trusted to be believed. You've got to be believed to be heard. And you've got to be
heard in order to persuade.

Whether you are selling a product, running for office, coaching a
sports team, commanding a platoon, giving a State of the Union address, preaching a sermon, or proposing marriage, you've got to get to
trust. The moment you begin to speak, your listener's First Brain is
watching you, studying your eye communication, reading your posture
and gestures, gauging your energy and enthusiasm—

And deciding whether or not to trust and believe you. Behavior
speaks louder than words, and you must get to trust or you'll get
nowhere.

In the next section, you'll learn how two visual principles—the Eye
Factor and the Energy Factor—are critical in establishing the trust you
need to communicate effectively.

Part III

Two Key Principles

The Six-Day Wonder: An Introduction to Your Personal Transformation

When Rich Casey came aboard as Syntex Corporation's new national sales manager, he was an unknown quantity in an uncertain situation. Energetic, aggressive, and extremely savvy at the tender age of thirty-three, Casey was viewed with a mixture of expectation, apprehension, and skepticism by the people at Syntex. Top management saw him as an up-and-comer, while old hands in the business saw him as a brash and brassy new kid on the block—just a flash in the pan.

A once thriving pharmaceutical giant, Palo Alto–based Syntex Corporation was going through hard times and needed a new infusion of energy and ideas. Its new wonder drug Naprosyn was hanging under a cloud, harmed by some earlier flawed studies. With the expected high growth rate retarded, Syntex could no longer rest on its past reputation. Rich Casey's job: Return this now lagging, sluggish pharmaceutical company to a robust and rambunctious force in the marketplace.

For the previous ten years, tall, lean, dark-haired Rich Casey had stood out in the field of four hundred Syntex salespeople. Suddenly a worried management had thrust him into the top sales job in the company, with orders to put Syntex back on the fast track. Could he do it? Some in the company thought so. Many others doubted. But most just didn't know who Rich Casey was or what kind of stuff he was made of. An atmosphere of "wait and see" hung over the organization. What everyone was waiting for was the National Sales Meeting at the Monterey Conference Center in Monterey, California, where the new national sales manager would be introduced.

Casey, who had been tapped for the position just three months before this crucial meeting, knew that his talk would be—for good or ill—the turning point of the meeting. It might well be the turning point of his career. It might even be the turning point of Syntex.

I met Rich Casey just six days before the conference was to begin. I knew his wife, Shelley, from a Decker Communications seminar she had taken six months earlier. A charming and gifted executive for Saga Corporation (now a division of Marriott), Shelley had enjoyed and benefited from her training in our program. She was sure Rich would benefit as well, since he had never seen himself on videotape before and was very apprehensive about his upcoming speech. Shelley urged Rich to take the program, but he was unable to find the time until it was almost too late.

With just six days to go before one of the biggest deadlines of his life, Rich was in my San Francisco office showing me the speech he had written. And it was a pretty good speech—on paper. I had Rich deliver his speech before a video camera, then had him watch the tape playback. The tape had only been rolling for a few minutes when he said, "My gosh! I had no idea I looked so stiff and boring when I give a speech! I can't go to the National Sales Meeting with that kind of presentation!"

I didn't have to say a word to convince him. Rich intuitively understood that his audience was going to be appraising his confidence, his competence, his ability to lead. They weren't going to be impressed by a man who lifelessly read a speech while standing behind a lectern, no matter how well written the speech was.

"Bert, what do I do?" Rich asked. "I'm facing an impossible challenge! I've only got a few days to reshape myself into a dazzling speaker and energize the entire sales force of my company! This is the most important presentation of my life—and I don't have time to memorize it! Help!"

"I wouldn't help you memorize it even if you *did* have time," I replied. "It would only sound as stiff and stilted as if you'd read it. But there is a better way."

For the next day and a half we worked on that "better way." Were we successful? Did Rich prevail over his "impossible challenge"? Was he able to convince the skeptics, energize his sales force, and turn the company around?

Well, let me just take you back to that autumn day in the Grand Ballroom of the Monterey Conference Center on the craggy coast of California. In contrast to the crisp, salty ocean-scented air outside, the room was hot and stuffy. Though the lights were low, people were perspiring—but no one was sweating that moment more than Rich Casey. The chairman of Syntex, Dr. Bert Bowers, finished his opening remarks, then turned to introduce the new national sales manager of the corporation. As his name was spoken, Rich stood and crossed the darkened stage, stepping into the small pool of light that haloed the lectern. The houselights came up, revealing an audience of several hundred men and women—the entire Syntex sales management team and most of its corporate officers. The applause was respectful, but brief. *Okay,* thought Rich Casey, *this is it!*

"This is a crucial moment for you, for our company, . . . and for me personally," he began. His wireless microphone picked up the keen intonation of his words, propelling them through the dense, stagnant air. "I've thought long and hard about the sales direction this company should take in the coming years, and about what I need to say to you this morning."

At that moment, Rich took up the manuscript of his speech, stepped out from behind the protective barrier of the lectern, and walked boldly to the center of the stage. "I wrote out a speech full of goals and objectives," he said, lifting the manuscript up, "but I got to thinking that maybe the most important thing for this company right now is not so much the goals and objectives for the next few months. What is important for us right now is the spirit that drives us. It's the spirit of each and every one of us. It's the spirit and vitality that is Syntex."

With a dramatic flourish, he ripped the speech from top to bottom.

"So let's forget the speech," he said as the pieces of the manuscript fluttered to the floor. "This morning I want to talk to you from the heart."

Then Rich Casey proceeded to give one of the most dramatic, powerful, and memorable talks Syntex had ever heard. Most of the ideas in that talk were the same ideas he had assembled in his written speech. But Rich delivered them with feeling, with spontaneity, with impact. In those few crucial moments, Rich Casey reached the First Brains of two hundred key people in his company.

Standing on the edge of the stage, moving easily from one side of the room to the other, he ceased to be a performer on a stage. He became a person. His listeners later remarked how he looked directly at each person in the room, how his eyes communicated with each individual. He stood tall and smiled easily (although, with his underlying nervousness, he certainly didn't feel like smiling). He gestured comfortably and confidently as he moved easily across the platform. His voice rose and fell dynamically, sometimes to underscore a point, sometimes to rivet attention, sometimes to convey emotion.

In those moments, Rich Casey did not merely give a speech. He became the leader of the Syntex sales force. He inspired his people to meet the challenge ahead with new energy and resolve. And, as people often do in the presence of genuine leadership and command, the audience gave Rich Casey a standing ovation.

Somewhere during the twenty-five or so minutes of Rich Casey's talk, the Syntex Corporation turned a corner. Naprosyn later grew from less than a hundred million to over half a billion in sales, and the sales force itself grew from four hundred to over a thousand. The career of Rich Casey would never be the same again. (He has since become the president of another biotech company.)

The story of Rich Casey is the story of a six-day wonder, an amazing personal transformation. Rich succeeded because he learned—in the nick of time!—how to reach the First Brain of his audience. He did it by emphasizing just two key principles.

And you can do the same.

Skeptical? By the end of the next two chapters, I expect to make a believer out of you.

Give us the tools, and we will finish the job.

Winston Churchill

Six Ways to Transform Your Personal Impact

In the Decker Program we have identified six skill areas that enable you to reach the First Brain of your listener. Each of these skills relates to two key principles—the Eye Factor and the Energy Factor.

These skills are simple to acquire and sharpen. That's why Rich Casey was able to transform himself as a communicator in only six days. If you focus on the visual impact of the Eye Factor and the personal dynamism of the Energy Factor, you'll be transformed too!

The two chapters of Part III are:

Chapter 6: *The Eye Factor*	*Chapter 7:* *The Energy Factor*
1. Eye Communication	5. Voice and Vocal Variety
2. Posture and Movement	6. Words and Nonwords (the Pause)
3. Dress and Appearance	
4. Gestures and the Smile	

CHAPTER 6

The Eye Factor

What you do speaks so loud I can't hear what you say. —Ralph Waldo Emerson

The Dominant Sense

My partner in founding Decker Communications was my late wife, Deborah. She was a lively, vital woman who fought a valiant three-year struggle with cancer. Although she lost the battle, her fight was an inspiration to all who knew her, particularly our three children.

Allison, Sam, and Ben were impressionable teenagers. Obviously, their mother was not herself at the end. The images of the last year were unflattering—and that was not the image of Deborah that I wanted the kids to have imprinted on their minds. So I took one of her typical laughing pictures, had it enlarged, and put it up in the family room right after the memorial service.

For months afterward, that three-by-four-foot picture of Deborah smiled down on us, a reminder of the person she was in the prime of life. Years later, that is still the image each of us carries in our memories of Deborah.

The visual sense is very powerful. The nerve pathways of the eye to the brain are twenty-five times larger than those from the ear to the brain. The eye is the only sensory organ that contains brain cells.

Memory experts invariably emphasize techniques that link the information you want to remember to a visual image. A huge body of research has been amassed demonstrating that out of all the brain's sensory input, it is the visual input that makes the greatest impact.

The nerve endings of our eyes are impacted by an estimated seven hundred thousand stimuli every instant. We cannot escape the massive visual bombardment of our brains. Psychologists have said that viewing an image three times has the power of one actual experience. This fact alone has enormous consequences for our movie and TV viewing habits. Imagine watching a grisly horror movie three or five or ten times. Imagine the destructive psychological and emotional impact on your mind from seeing human beings murdered in fiendish ways again and again. It would have the same effect on your mind as being an eyewitness to a series of brutal murders!

The visual sense dominates *all* of the senses. The visual channel communicates with power and impact. To communicate effectively in today's business and social worlds, you must be aware of the language of the First Brain, which is a visual language. Most important of all, you must learn to *use* this language fluently and effectively.

The Inconsistent Message

A spoken message is made up of three components: verbal, vocal, and visual. In his book *Silent Messages,* Professor Albert Mehrabian of UCLA described his landmark study on the relationships between the "Three Vs" of spoken communication. He measured the effect that each of these three components has on the believability of a message.

The verbal element is the message itself—the words you say. Most of us tend to concentrate only on the verbal element, mistakenly assuming this to be the *entire* message, when in fact it is only *part* of the message.

The second part of the message is the vocal element—the intonation, projection, and resonance of your voice as it carries the words.

The third part is the visual element—what people see, the motion and expression of your body and face as you speak.

Professor Mehrabian's research found that the degree of consistency (or inconsistency) between these three elements is the factor that determines the believability of your message. The more these three factors harmonize with each other, the more believable you are as a speaker.

Let's do an experiment: Write your estimate of the percentage of impact each element has on the believability of your message:

What happens when these three components contradict each other? We transmit an inconsistent message. We literally send out mixed signals. Which signals will our listeners find the most convincing? Which signals will our listeners believe? Which will they ignore?

In his research, Albert Mehrabian found that when we send out an inconsistent message, our verbal content is virtually smothered by vocal and visual components. Just look at his results:

What Counts: *Believability*

Verbal	————
Vocal	————
Visual	————
Total	100%

How did Mehrabian's actual results compare with your estimate? Were you surprised? Yet it's absolutely true! Vocal and visual communication trump the verbal. When the vocal and visual components of our message are inconsistent with the verbal content, people believe the vocal and visual—and reject the verbal. Result: We are simply not believed. Our message fails to get through.

But when all three components combine into a totally consistent message, we are not only believable, *we have impact*. The excitement and enthusiasm of your voice work with the energy and animation of your face and body to reflect the conviction of your message. When all three components work together in harmony, you reach your listener's First Brain—and *persuasion* takes place.[1]

What does the visual channel tell the listener about us when we send out an inconsistent message? Perhaps it says we are insincere or dishonest. Or that we lack confidence. Or have something to hide.

WYSIWYG is a computer term that stands for "What You See Is What You Get." It applies to personal impact as well. The message you see is the message you get. Clearly, the primary path to First-Brain believability is the visual channel. How, then, do we use visual elements to enhance rather than inhibit our message?

Why Use Visual Aids When You Speak?

- Various studies show that retention increases from 14 percent to 38 percent when listeners see as well as hear a speaker's message.
- Speaker's goals are met 34 percent more often when visuals are used than when they are not.
- Group consensus occurs 21 percent more often in meetings with visuals than in those without.
- Time required to present a concept can be reduced up to 40 percent with the use of visuals.
- When visuals were used in teaching a course on vocabulary, learning improved 200 percent.

What Counts: *Believability*

Verbal	————	7%
Vocal	————	38%
Visual	————	55%
Total		100%

1. Eye Communication

An eye can threaten like a loaded and leveled gun; or can insult like hissing and kicking; or in its altered mood by beams of kindness, make the heart dance with joy.

Ralph Waldo Emerson

Eye communication is your number one skill. It ranks first because it has the greatest impact in both one-on-one communications and large group communications. It literally connects mind to mind, since your eyes are the only part of your central nervous system that is in direct contact with another human being. When your eyes meet the eyes of another person, you make a First-Brain-to-First-Brain connection. When you fail to make that connection, it matters very little what you say.

EXAMPLES

- Judy Sandler is an outside salesperson for a major corporation. She has a problem with "eye-dart." Even in casual conversations, her eyes flit about like those of a high-strung thoroughbred filly. When

"Eye-dart"

"Slo-blink"

she talks with clients or her peers on the sales force, her eye-dart goes into high gear. Result: She comes across as shifty and untrustworthy. She fails to connect with her listeners' First Brain—and sales that could have been hers go to the competition.

• Marion James is a personnel director for a major corporation. When she interviews people, she rarely looks them in the eye, and often gazes out the window while talking. This unconscious habit makes her appear uninterested and distant.

• Doug Thomas is the minister of a small church. In the pulpit, he often closes his eyes for two or three seconds while speaking. Perhaps he is unconsciously imitating the behavior of another pastor he admires, but this habit makes him appear aloof. Worse, it carries over into his personal conversations. His parishioners see him as cold and detached—the exact opposite of the way Doug sees himself.

Do you see yourself in these examples? If so there's hope. Eye communication problems are curable. Don't assume that making occasional, glancing eye contact is enough. Good eye communication is more than a glance. True eye communication involves using your eyes to make a First-Brain-to-First-Brain connection.

THE BASIC RULES

Use involvement rather than intimacy or intimidation. Intimacy and intimidation both involve looking at another person steadily for long periods—say, ten seconds to a minute or more. In business and normal social conversations, both intimacy and intimidation make listeners feel uncomfortable. But over 90 percent of our business and social communications call for involvement. How do you achieve that "just right" level of eye connection that conveys a feeling of involvement?

For effective eye communication, count to five. A feeling of involvement requires about five seconds of steady eye contact. That's about the time we take to complete a thought or a sentence. When we talk to another person and are excited, enthusiastic, and confident, we usually look at them for five to ten seconds before looking away. That's natural and comfortable for most listeners in one-on-one communications, so it's logical that we should try to meet that expectation in all our speaking situations, whether we are addressing one listener or a roomful. Push for longer eye communication—beyond your comfort zone. It's easy to revert to short eye-contact habits unless you work at it.

Beware of eye-dart. When we are under pressure or feel anxious, our instinct is to avoid the eyes of our listeners. Unfortunately, the listener can read that anxiety in our darting eyes. We give the appearance of a scared rabbit. We exude the scent of fear—and our lack of confidence undermines our credibility.

Beware of slo-blink. On the other hand, it's equally disconcerting to talk to a person with the slo-blink habit. This is where a person closes his or her eyes for up to two or three seconds while speaking. This habit conveys the message "I really don't want to be here." It doesn't take long before our listeners feel the same way.

114

SOME BASIC EXERCISES

Get video feedback. To make yourself aware of your eye movements—both length of contact and idiosyncrasies like eye-dart or slo-blink—have someone tape you while you are making a presentation. Practice in your company's training room, take a video feedback course, or do it at home. (See www.deckercommunications.com.)

Practice one-on-one at every opportunity. Ask a friend to keep track of your eye patterns during a normal conversation. Have your friend silently count while you make eye contact, and record it so that he or she can tell you later. Then get an average count on how long you tend to look at a person. Work on pushing that average to five seconds or more.

Practice with a paper audience. When you have a presentation coming up, draw happy faces on Post-it notes—or, if you prefer, unhappy faces (tough audience)—and stick those notes on chairs or on the wall in the room where you practice your talk. Put a face at each "fringe," or edge of the audience, next to the corner.

Now give your presentation to your paper audience. Talk to the chairs or wall—the whole wall, corner to corner. Practice your movement, too (see below). Be sure to give at least five seconds of eye contact to each face, and be sure to include the faces at the fringes.

Watch the TV news. Increase your awareness and "eye savvy" by seeing real people in pressure situations. Observe people being themselves, attempting to persuade while under pressure. Note their eye communication patterns. Watch shows like *60 Minutes* or *20/20* where people are put on the defensive and the heat is on. The First Brain reveals itself in eye communication. Notice telltale signs of fear, anger, arrogance, evasion, or sadness in the eyes. Look for signs of confidence and believability. See how eye communication can enhance or betray a person's credibility and likability.

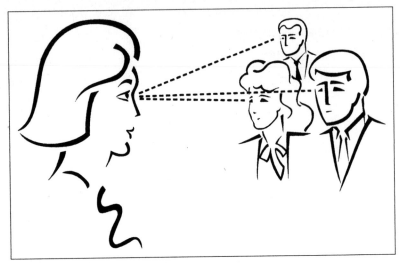

At least five seconds of eye contact

THE BENEFITS OF GOOD EYE COMMUNICATION

- You feel less nervous (like having a series of one-on-one conversations with people).
- You appear confident (whether you are or not).
- You focus your thoughts.
- You can motivate your movement.
- You "read" your audience by seeing individuals.

Remember: Contact eyes, not faces. Look at people for four, five, or six seconds. And concentrate particularly on eliminating rapid and/or distracting eye movements.

A Vietnam Soldier:
Eye Contact Saved His Life

He began by telling about being a soldier in Vietnam. One evening he and his buddies were pinned down in a bunker. His fellow soldiers were killed and he was hit three times—once each in his right shoulder, his right thigh, and his left side.

Lying on the ground, he thought that any moment he'd die. He visualized his heart pumping all the blood out of his left side . . . and then just quitting . . . and he'd be dead.

About that time the Vietcong soldiers came up and started going through the dead American soldiers' bodies, taking their valuables—watches, rings, money, even knocking gold fillings out of their teeth.

One of the soldiers came up to him, reached down for his watch, and discovered he was still alive when the young man jerked his hand away. Immediately the enemy soldier pointed his gun between the young man's eyes. The young man knew he was about to die.

He told how he looked up into the soldier's eyes, with as much feeling and emotion as he could muster, shook his head from side to side, and said, "No . . . no . . . please don't kill me!"

After a moment the enemy soldier could no longer handle it emotionally, broke eye contact, and pulled his gun away. Just then another Vietcong soldier yelled something. The young man assumed he asked if he was still alive, because the soldier yelled something back, which he assumed was "Yes." Then the other soldier yelled again. My friend assumed he yelled, "Kill him!" because once again the soldier pointed his gun at him and was about to pull the trigger.

Again, the young man looked deeply into his enemy's eyes, nodded his head from side to side, and said, "No . . . no . . . please don't kill me . . . please don't."

After an incredibly painful pause, even though he couldn't understand the language, the Vietcong soldier once again backed down, broke eye contact, pulled his gun away, pointed it into the ground a few feet away, and pulled the trigger. He then yelled something to the other soldier, and walked away.

From *Integrity Selling* by Ron Willingham[2]

2. Posture and Movement

Stand tall. The difference between towering and cowering is totally a matter of inner posture. It's got nothing to do with height, it costs nothing and it's more fun.

Malcolm Forbes

Confidence is best expressed through good, upright posture. How you hold yourself physically is an indicator of how you hold yourself mentally—and a decisive factor in how others regard you.

EXAMPLES

- Phyllis Manning runs her own consulting firm. She thought she had a big tummy as a little girl, so she consciously sucked in her stomach at all times. This caused her shoulders to go back, so that as an adult she has very erect body posture. Because of the confident way she walks, she commands attention when she enters a room.

- Denise Elliot was a typical seventeen-year-old. She was in the audience when I appeared on the "SFO Evening Magazine" television show to demonstrate the impact of our video seminars. Denise volunteered to give an impromptu on-camera talk, then participate in the Decker Program. The following week, she would return to the show and talk on-camera again—a live "before-and-after" experiment.

   In the "before" segment she talked rapidly—a lot of *um*s and *ah*s, a few giggles, the kind of nervousness you'd expect from a first solo performance before a TV audience. She slumped a little, with her weight on her left hip, arms akimbo—a stance that gave her an anxious, insecure look. Could Denise dramatically improve her habits and her posture before next week's show?

   She completed the two-day training on the afternoon of the live broadcast. She kept saying how nervous she was—and I wondered if this live demonstration would turn out to be a disaster for her and for me! My company and I had a lot of credibility riding on the performance of this seventeen-year-old girl.

   I went out first to explain to the audience what we had done. Then Denise strode from behind the curtain and stood tall and composed on the stage. Before she opened her mouth, her posture exuded an almost tangible assurance. She was terrific—and she made me look good, too!

People form impressions of us in the first few seconds after they meet us. They make assumptions about our attitude, our confidence, our competence, even our rank and position. Many people have posture habits that undermine trust and convey a lack of self-assurance. Even if you inwardly feel confident, poor posture will invariably communicate a lack of poise. The good news is that there are some simple things you can do to improve your posture habits.

THE BASIC RULES

Stand tall. Poor upper body posture often reflects low self-esteem. Stand with your shoulders back and your stomach in. Visualize a string rising from the center of your scalp like a candle wick, pulling you upward. Whether you are walking into a room or speaking before an audience, stand straight (but not starchy) and move naturally. Remain fluid rather than locked into a rigid position. You'll make a visual impact.

Watch your lower body. The lower body is the neglected aspect of good posture. One common posture problem for speakers is going

Back on one hip

back on one hip. You actually lean away from your audience and communicate, "I don't want to be here." This is true both in presentations and in casual conversations. Variations include rocking from side to side or going forward and back from heel to toe.

Get in the "Ready Position." The Ready Position means basically weight forward. Communication rides on energy, and your posture either communicates energy and enthusiasm—or apathy and disinterest. When you speak confidently from a self-assured stance, your energy is directed forward, physically and psychologically, toward your listener. The Ready Position looks like this: Lean slightly forward, knees somewhat flexed, so you can bounce lightly on the balls of your feet. You should feel like an athlete ready to move quickly in any direction. When your weight is forward, it's impossible to go back on one hip or rock on your heels.

Move. Tradition says that speakers should always be rooted to one spot when they speak. Well, tradition is wrong! To make emotional contact with our listeners, we need to convey excitement, enthusiasm, and confidence when we speak. That means we've gotta move! Motion is visual! Motion is energetic! How can we move people to action when we are standing still?

Think of the lectern as the eight-ball. Don't get trapped behind it! Get rid of any physical barriers between yourself and your audience. Move around and gesture freely. Movement adds energy and variety to your message and imbues you with an aura of confidence.

Move naturally, a few steps at a time, rather than taking a single tentative one-step. With eye communication motivating you, take a few natural steps toward one person, pause as you complete your thought, then move on to another set of eyes. Beware of repetitive and mechanical movements that are worse than standing still.

SOME BASIC EXERCISES

Do the Miss America Exercise, or walk away from the wall. Have you ever seen a Miss America pageant? Ever notice the fabulous posture

Trapped by tradition

of every contestant? Former Miss America Donna Axum once told me about an exercise almost every contestant uses for good posture. It's simple, and you can gain from it.

Find a bare wall in your home or office. Set your heels against the wall. Then set your shoulders against the wall. Then your rear. Now comes the hard part: Press as much of the small of your back as you can against the wall. You should be ramrod straight.

Now walk away from the wall, and give a slight shake. How do you feel as you step away from the wall? Straight as a telephone pole? Probably. And you look good. You have great posture—but you're not *too* stiff.

Videotape yourself before and after the Miss America Exercise. You'll be convinced. You *can* improve your posture. Practice this exercise and use it before giving a presentation.

Use the Ready Position in all situations. Make the Ready Position a habit so that when you speak, you don't even have to think about your posture. The Ready Position will be ingrained in you.

The Ready Position

Begin the Two-Step. In our training programs we find that many people resist coming out from behind the lectern. Some take a tentative step to one side—then they take root. That doesn't do it. You have to do the Two-Step.

The Two-Step is simply a technique to help us remember to take at least two full steps—then keep moving. The Two-Step won't let you get away with halfhearted movements. It forces you to move toward someone at the side or in the middle of the audience. It forces you to direct your kinetic energy forward. Get in the habit of using your energy. Do the Two-Step.

View your posture and movement on video. The most definitive form of feedback is video feedback. A camcorder sees all, tells all. As you push yourself to stand straighter, focus your energy forward, and move toward people in a more open way, you will actually see that it doesn't look as exaggerated as it feels. Video feedback will help you become comfortable with your new posture and movement habits. Video feedback is the best way to get an objective look at your communicating behavior.

THE BENEFITS OF GOOD POSTURE AND MOVEMENT

- You feel taller and more powerful.
- You look more confident.
- Your movement makes eye communication easier (they work together).
- Your habit of being forward in the Ready Position helps you be psychologically forward.
- Your movement gives variety to the eye of the audience.

Remember: Stand tall; use the Ready Position; focus on "energy forward." Most of all, get out from behind the lectern and move!

3. Dress and Appearance

You never get a second chance to make a good first impression.

John Molloy

After posture, the most immediate visual impression we make on our listener's First Brain comes from our dress and appearance. I have a theory that I call the two-by-four rule, which has been validated in the experience of training thousands of people: The impressions made in the first two seconds are so vivid that it takes another four minutes to add another 50 percent more impression (negative or positive) to that communication. And those first two seconds are almost entirely visual, made up of how we look. This means that if we make a poor first impression, even before we open our mouth, it takes a really long time to overcome any damage done.

THE ODD COUPLE

Years ago, my son Ben and I spent a hot, noisy summer day at the Taste of Chicago in Grant Park. Up and down Lake Shore Drive, along Lake Michigan, foods from every country and culture imaginable were sold and consumed against a background of music and fun.

Even in that funky, variegated crowd, one couple stood out. The

The Odd Couple

young man had a neon-orange Mohawk, two inches wide and two feet high, swooping halfway down his back. His head was shaved at the sides and a gold hoop earring dangled from one ear. His black leather jacket was festooned with colorful braids and silver studs.

His girlfriend was more than a match for him. Half of her face was garishly greasepainted in a clash of Day-Glo colors. The other side of her face had no makeup whatsoever. She wore a skimpy, see-through halter top. This couple wanted attention—and they got it.

Ben and I followed them around for about fifteen minutes—not just to watch *them* but to watch *other* people watching them. It was fascinating. As people approached, they were careful not to stare. But as soon as they passed the couple's line of sight, they turned and gawked in wonder. I know we're taught that it's not polite to stare—but in that situation, staring was practically mandatory!

Our appearance communicates who we are—our values, our self-image, our self-respect. That garish duo on Lake Shore Drive was making a statement about themselves. And how we dress for a speaking event makes a statement, too. It sends a message.

Our dress and appearance can make (or break) an emotional connection with our listeners. We should dress and groom in such a way that our appearance is appropriate to who we are—and to the values and culture of our listeners.

EXAMPLES

- Back in my film-producing days I usually sported the casual, tieless "uniform" of a filmmaker. Today I'm embarrassed to think of the reaction some people must have had to me. I vividly remember the time I spoke before fifty top managers of *Sunset* magazine, selling a film concept to this notably conservative company. I wore a plaid sports jacket, a solid black knit tie, and a dazzling red shirt printed with silhouettes of women dancing under swaying palms. Somehow, I got the job and made the film—but to this day I wonder how I overcame what must have been a very negative First-Brain impression!

- Paul Green is a personnel expert and the head of Behavioral Technology of Memphis. He travels the country, speaking and training on matters of hiring and firing. Two decades ago, Paul pioneered a look that has become fashionable today: Paul shaved his head. "My hair was thinning," he said, "and I consciously decided to go all the way. It was truly one of the best decisions I ever made. I look better, and people remember me."

- My friend Guy Kawasaki, CEO of Garage Technology Ventures, is a busy public speaker who gives two or three speeches a week. In his blog (http://blog.guykawasaki.com/), Guy writes, "My father was a politician in Hawaii. He was a very good speaker. When I started speaking he gave me a piece of advice: Never dress beneath the level of the audience. That is, if they're wearing suits, then you should wear a suit. To underdress is to communicate the following message: 'I'm smarter/richer/more powerful than you. I can insult you and not take you serious, and there's nothing you can do about it.' This is hardly the way to get an audience to like you."

THE BASIC RULES

Be Appropriate. There is not so much a right or wrong way to dress as there is an appropriate way. This means you should, first, be appropriate to your environment and, second, be appropriate to yourself. Dress to be comfortable with yourself and to make others comfortable with you. Cultivate a style that allows you to feel relaxed, but that accommodates flexibly to the norms of the group, the social setting, the time of day, and the weather. Some tips for appropriateness:

- Conservative is better for business.
- Dress up, not down. It's safer to be overdressed than underdressed.
- Women: If in doubt about a pantsuit, don't. A suit, dress, or skirt and blouse are fine in almost all business settings.
- Pick two or three basic colors that look good on you, and stay with those basics. Let accessories (scarves, ties) provide the accents.
- If you know you'll be speaking in a corporate culture that prizes informality instead of dress codes (remember the early days at Apple?), ignore these tips and go with the culture.

Make conscious choices. Don't get stuck in a rut. Take an objective, conscious look at how you dress and groom. Are you still wearing the ties you wore in college? Is that jewelry still effective or is it time to experiment? Are you sure that haircut still works for you? Your appearance instantly communicates how you feel about yourself—and your audience. Put some serious thought into it.

Button your jacket. Buttoned generally looks better. True, some women's suits are tailored to be unbuttoned—but *all* men's suits and jackets are tailored to be buttoned when you want to look smart.

SOME BASIC EXERCISES

Get feedback. Style is subjective. It pays to find out what others think of you. So ask for opinions about your visual aspect. Men: Ask for feedback on clothing, hair, beard, mustache, accents, and jewelry. Women: Ask for feedback on clothing and accents, hairstyle, makeup, and jewelry. Consider the appropriateness of your fragrance. Seek honest appraisals from a variety of people.

Be observant. Read current magazines on style. Observe your coworkers and friends. Notice who is on the fast track. Learn—but don't be a carbon copy. Develop your own unique style.

Test out your first two seconds. Remember that people form important impressions of you in the first two seconds after meeting you. Those impressions are primarily from your dress and appearance. Find out what people think by asking them.

THE BENEFITS OF GOOD DRESS AND APPEARANCE
- You feel confident in how you look.
- You take less time dressing and grooming when you know what you are doing, and why.
- You make a positive impression that adds to your effectiveness (and you don't have to overcome a negative first impression).

To button, or not to button

- You can more easily make positive changes in your dress and appearance than any other skill, and thus gain immediate benefit.

  Remember: Be appropriate, be conscious, and be smart.

4. Gestures and the Smile

We don't "know" our presidents. We imagine them. We watch them intermittently and from afar, inferring from only a relatively few gestures and reactions what kind of people they are and whether they should be in charge. Much depends on our intuition and their ability at a handful of opportune moments to project qualities we admire and respect. —Meg Greenfield

Looking good

Your listener's First Brain is wary and watchful. It's looking for the nonverbal cues that prove you can be believed and trusted. The First Brain knows that if we believe what we are saying, we will be animated while we are saying it.

When you communicate, are you enthused? Excited? Do you speak with conviction and passion? Your listener's First Brain wants to know not just what you are saying, but how you *feel* about what you are saying. It's measuring the Eye Factor—those visual cues that communicate your emotional state.

There are few things that do more for effective communication than open gestures and a warm open smile. Your smile dominates your listener's impression of you. A smile shows not only on your mouth but in your eyes. It demonstrates openness and likability.

Gestures and smiles are the dominant visual components of spoken communication. Our gestures and smiles reveal our inner state and propel our message with energy and emotional force.

EXAMPLES

• Ted Mallard had a problem with gestures. He went through the Decker Program, where he was videotaped giving his opening two-minute introduction. He started with a classic nervous gesture called the "fig leaf." Then he switched to something much worse. Every few seconds he would raise his cupped hands for a moment, then drop

"Fig leaf flasher"

them back into the "fig leaf " position. When he saw the effect later on video playback, he called himself "the fig leaf flasher." He made it a point to drop this habit and build some new gestures into his speaking repertoire.

- Charles Levitt was the senior VP of a major advertising agency. His employees considered him grim and unapproachable. At home, his kids sometimes asked him, "What's wrong, Dad?" Inwardly, he felt fine! Why did people think something was wrong? When he went through the Decker Program and saw himself on videotape, he finally understood. He never smiled! So he tried a smile on video—and it looked good. He even exaggerated his smile. It looked great—not exaggerated at all! From then on, Charles Levitt made it a point to wear a smile on his face and let the world know that he felt great, he was full of energy and enthusiasm, and he was friendly and approachable.

You want to be a natural communicator, so relax! Keep your arms at your sides when you are at rest. Then, when your message calls for animation, enthusiasm, and underscoring, gesture naturally.

Learn to smile under pressure. Cultivate the same natural smile when you're on the hot seat as when you kick back with friends.

Your gestures and smile will demonstrate whether you are open or closed to your listeners. It's a truth as old as the Old Testament: "He who would have friends, let him show himself friendly" (Proverbs 18:24).

THE BASIC RULES

Find your nervous gesture—and stop it! We all have nervous gestures. We all have a place our hands seem to stray to whenever we feel anxious and need to hold on to something. To find your nervous gesture, give a short talk before a video camera. Once you're aware of it, avoid it. Focus on keeping your hands naturally at your sides until you need them to emphasize an emotion or a point. When you need them, the gestures will come naturally. But you can't gesture naturally when your hands are locked in a "fig leaf " or some other nervous gesture.

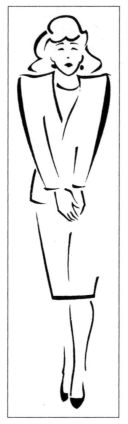

"Fig leaf"

Give yourself permission to exaggerate. It's very hard to really exaggerate your communicating energy. There's a huge disparity between how we perceive our gestures and expressions and how others perceive them. A woman with a naturally unsmiling face may think she's beaming with joy—yet others around her think, *What's she so glum about?*

Smile—then push your smile. Make it broader and brighter. Then push it a bit more. You may think you're making a grinning fool of yourself—but others will just see a warm, natural, pleasing smile.

We have an exercise in our communication workshop called the Disparity Exercise. It enables people to experiment with exaggerations that feel uncomfortable but that truly appear natural to the outside

"Napoleon"

observer. You can try the Disparity Exercise yourself. Get in front of a camcorder and try to exaggerate your smile, your gestures, your personal energy. Don't worry about overdoing it—*try* to overdo it! Then rewind the tape and see yourself as others see you. I guarantee you'll be surprised at how normal and natural you appear.

Find out which third you're in. We all think we smile much of the time. In reality, the people around us may view us quite differently—and it's their opinion that counts. Experience from the thousands of people in our training programs has shown that approximately one-third of us have naturally open and smiling faces. Another third have neutral faces that can readily go from a smile to a serious look. The

"Prayer Position"

"lower third" have faces that are naturally serious (if not downright grim!)—even when they think they're smiling.

Find out which third you're in. Ask people for their honest assessment—or better yet, get video feedback, the most objective feedback of all. If you're in the top third of smilers, you have a built-in advantage in your communication with others. People will naturally perceive you as open and friendly, and be more open to your ideas.

If you're in the neutral third, you have flexibility—but you should be conscious from moment to moment of the energy level and enthusiasm your face registers.

If you're in the bottom third—the "grim group"—you have your assignment: Exaggerate! Practice your smile in front of a mirror or camcorder. Ask your spouse or a friend to tickle your ribs whenever

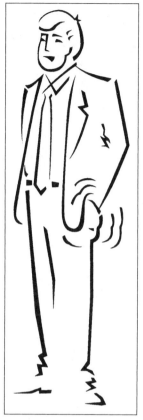

"Jangler"

your face sags. Make yourself conscious, moment by moment, of what your facial muscles are doing. And remember, you're not alone. I have a grim exterior myself. Unless I'm consciously working at it, my face projects a low-energy, stern appearance—even when I'm grinning from ear to ear inside! I have to work at letting my inner energy show through my face—and you may have to as well.

"Lift your apples." There's nothing mysterious about a smile, except the magical effect it has on others. A smile is the result of the physical operation of facial muscles, and these muscles can be exercised. The best way to practice smiling is not by moving your lips to form a smile. Think rather of raising your cheekbones. Consider the upper part of your cheeks as apples and just "lift your apples" to smile.

"Lift your apples"

Your smile affects you. Your smile not only affects others; it also has an effect on you—physically. When you smile, you feel it throughout your body. People can also hear your smile in your voice—so you should smile whenever you speak, even when you're on the phone. People may not see your smile over the phone, but they'll definitely hear it.

Caution: Phony smiles don't work. A great smile should reveal how you feel inside—but don't paste on a phony smile. Fake smiles *look* fake. Instead, train your facial muscles to smile naturally—and never forget: A true smile comes from within.

SOME BASIC EXERCISES

Practice exaggeration. Exaggerate your smile, facial expressions, and gestures. Try it in the mirror or on videotape. You'll defuse your inhibitions as you discover that what *feels* exaggerated does not really *look* exaggerated. Experiment and practice your exaggerated communication skills in private—then try them out in your public speaking opportunities and see what a difference those skills make. Soon, your "exaggerated" skills will seem natural and normal to you.

Try a winger. A winger is an impromptu presentation. Talk about your favorite hobby or your favorite book for five minutes. As you talk, observe how your hands and arms move. Do they stray to an inhibited position, such as the "fig leaf," or do they stay lifelessly at your sides the whole time? Practice using gestures to communicate energy and passion about your subject.

Get big. As you practice gestures, look for phrases and concepts in your talk that demand bigger gestures. Look for ideas that are so big that you can only convey them by reaching for the ceiling, stretching your arms out wide, putting kinetic energy into your motions, and

"Get big"

physically moving from wall to wall. As you try to put bigger gestures into your talk, your mind will gravitate toward bigger, more dynamic ideas. The content of your message will become more powerful and fascinating—and you'll have much more impact as a speaker.

Imitate an "expressor." Pick an expressive, high-energy public figure to serve as your role model—then try to imitate that person. Toss your inhibitions aside. Try to get inside the skin of that person and play the part with gusto. Who's your idea of a dynamic, high-energy role model? Some ideas: Oprah. Robin Williams. Mick Jagger. Robert Schuller. John Madden. Jesse Jackson. Tom Peters. Steve Irwin. Zig Ziglar. Try to become that energetic, expressive person, and you'll unleash the hidden energy in your own personality.

THE BENEFITS OF GOOD GESTURES AND THE SMILE

- You are free to express your thoughts fully.
- Smile—and the world smiles with you.
- Your natural energy can be released.
- Your open gestures *show* your openness—your willingness to listen as well as talk.
- You can use gestures to emphasize ideas and underscore emotions.

Remember: Put movement and energy into your gestures. If you are shy and low-key, then make a special effort to exaggerate your communicating energy. Push your smile. Use big gestures—but stay within your natural energy level (no jumping on Oprah's couch!). Genuine enthusiasm wins trust, but affected, unnatural gestures make you seem artificial and insincere.

To summarize, the first four of the six ways to transform your personal impact are:

1. Eye Communication
2. Posture and Movement
3. Dress and Appearance
4. Gestures and the Smile

"Yes"

The Eye Factor rules! The visual sense dominates *all* the senses. The language of the First Brain is a visual language. Learn to speak this visual language and you *will* make emotional contact, you *will* gain your listeners' trust—

And you'll be effective and persuasive every time you speak.

CHAPTER 7

The Energy Factor

The Secret of Bobby Kennedy

Robert F. Kennedy was not a great communicator in the classic sense. He certainly did not possess the natural oratorical skills of his brother John. Yet there was something about Bobby that worked. When he spoke, he made contact with his audience. He had energy—and he used it.

I got to watch Bobby Kennedy in action—behind the scenes as well as onstage in front of the cameras—as a twenty-eight-year-old film director. I was young and not too experienced. I just happened to be in the right place at the right time to observe a piece of history. And though I hardly knew it then, the seeds of the First-Brain concept were already being planted in my mind as I watched this legendary man at work.

It was an unusually hot spring night for Washington when I got the phone call at home that plunged me into the dizzying whirl of Kennedy's 1968 presidential campaign. The call was from my boss, Charles Guggenheim, the renowned Academy Award–winning documentary filmmaker. He wanted to see me at the office. "Immediately," he said, and that was not like Charles. When I arrived, he spoke quickly. "Bobby Kennedy just threw his hat in the ring. He's picked California for the first leg of the campaign. I want you to put together a couple of film crews and follow him everywhere he goes."

Guggenheim Productions had been contracted to produce Kennedy's TV commercials. Our job was to get everything on film so it could all be edited down to a series of thirty- and sixty-second spots and short films. I hastily assembled the film crews, and the next thing I knew we were on the press plane, part of a three-jet entourage winging through eight California cities in three days.

Kennedy was a fascinating man to watch. I have to confess that I wasn't a big RFK fan at first. But as I watched him—in closed-door meetings, before the press, grabbing a few moments of rest, delivering his stump speech, shaking who knows how many outstretched hands—I became intrigued with the energy that flowed from him. It was not so much his message that impressed me, but the extraordinary personal impact with which he delivered it. He clearly made a powerful impression on every person he touched.

Certainly, there were times when his style struck my First Brain as abrasive and abrupt, which gave resonance to the charge of "ruthlessness" that was circulating about him. But the communicative power of his presence seemed to excite everyone—both his staff and the crowds who flocked to hear him. Amazingly, even those who disagreed with his politics seemed as deeply affected by Kennedy's persona as those who supported him.

In city after city, our cameras captured every word, gesture, and nuance. Soon it dawned on me that I was seeing something that was definitely not what is ordinarily described as "charisma." That hypnotic, spellbinding quality that surrounds most so-called charismatic speakers just didn't fit Bobby Kennedy. His delivery was much more down-to-earth, much more subtle and real. His was almost an entirely new brand of communication.

Kennedy's speaking style broke every rule. His pronounced Boston accent and halting delivery would have been a fatal handicap for most speakers, yet he somehow turned his eccentricities into assets. Many years later, in a *Newsweek* article, Meg Greenfield would make a similar observation about Bobby's brother John, reflecting that "he managed to retain and impose his stylistic eccentricities on the public consciousness—he wore what he wore and spoke the funny 'Cube-er' way he spoke. So he established authenticity and then, in the first debate, he established that his personality was that of a leader, a plausible president."

Throughout that grueling jet tour through California in the spring of 1968, I saw Kennedy repeatedly face all the incredible pressures and frustrations of the campaign trail: last-minute schedule changes, inadequate accommodations, malfunctioning sound systems, staff conflicts, and hostile questioners. Yet he never lost the ability to put himself across in that amazing way that was his style alone.

Near the end of that tour, I saw the Kennedy energy tested to the limit.

It was another hot spring night as Kennedy approached the podium in front of the California State Capitol in Sacramento. To me, it seemed the man had been squeezed dry by the pressure and the pace. As he walked, his legs literally shook from exhaustion. I was a couple of feet away, watching him take his place before the vast milling crowd. I wondered how he could pull himself together for one more delivery of what had essentially been the same speech in city after city. I was exhausted myself, short on temper, wanting nothing more than to go somewhere and sleep—and I was just a guy in the entourage. But Kennedy had been under continuous pressure and nerve-racking scrutiny the whole time—and the dream of a whole lifetime was on the line. I couldn't imagine how he summoned the gumption for each new speech, meeting, and TV interview.

As our cameras rolled, I thought, *Look at him! There's no way he can make it! He can barely stay on his feet!*

But as soon as he was introduced, something happened to him. He seemed to spring forward, evoking the image of a runner sprinting from the blocks or a fighter coming out of his corner. All evidence of his exhaustion was erased from his face. His legs still trembled, but few people were aware of it. Within moments, he propelled himself into one of the most effective speeches of the tour. A speech filled with passion. With power. With energy.

Our crews captured some of the most memorable footage of the entire tour during those moments.

Three months after that tour, Kennedy was well on his way to winning the Democratic nomination for president of the United States when he was fatally wounded by an assassin's bullet at the Los Angeles Ambassador Hotel. From what I saw of Kennedy as a leader and a communicator, I'm convinced that, were it not for that bullet, the history of our nation would have been written very differently.

Reflecting on those memories of Bobby Kennedy, I can clearly understand why this man consistently got to the heart of his listeners. His sheer use of personal energy enabled him to connect with the First Brains of his listeners. He was a master at using humor, unforgettable language, and personal involvement to connect with his audience. There was energy in his voice, but even more so in his face and in his body language. The vocal and visual power of the man conveyed to the millions who saw him in person and on TV that here is a man who believes what he says. A line of narration from Guggenheim Productions' Academy Award–winning film, *Robert Kennedy Remembered,* captures it well: "He entered the Senate in characteristic style—leaning forward." People respond to that kind of conviction. That's why people responded to Bobby Kennedy.

His best asset as a speaker was his energy. And there is simply nothing mysterious or magical about energy. It's a dynamic quality that anyone can use to reach and persuade his or her listeners. Spoken without energy, the most eloquent and profound words in the world will be instantly forgotten. But even an average person with ordinary credentials can get people to respond to him and even follow him *if he has energy when he speaks!*

The Best Teacher

Not convinced? Then let's try a little experiment. Think back to your high school and college days. Now think quickly: Who was the *best* teacher you ever had?

I've asked this question of literally thousands of people, and almost without exception people instantly flash on a certain type of teacher.

And it is not necessarily the teacher with the most impressive degrees, or most published works, or even the teacher who was best prepared and most knowledgeable.

The teacher who stands out as the *best* in our minds is almost always the teacher who had *energy,* who was interesting to listen to, who had dynamic and creative ways of getting the message across. It's the teacher who was the most excited, enthused, and eager for you to get the information and principles from the class. It's the teacher with a big extra ingredient I call the "Energy Factor."

When I was at Yale I had to take a History of Art course to satisfy a requirement—and I liked neither history nor art. The morning of the first class, I approached Woolsey Hall with a cloud of ennui over my head, dreading the next fifty minutes of unrelieved tedium. The auditorium was dimly lit—perfect for catching up on the sleep I had missed the night before. In fact, I was just beginning to doze when Professor Vincent Scully walked into the spotlight. Yes, a spotlight. For Vincent Scully had no intention of letting anyone sleep in his class!

His voice rang out as he announced the importance of this course. Without a pause he flashed the first slide on the screen, strode across the stage, and used his pointer to bang against the screen, making his points. He roamed the stage like a restless tiger as he drove home to each student in that room the subtle intricacies and nuances of each painting, sculpture, or architectural design. It didn't matter what medium, or what artistic period, or what artist he was talking about— this man knew how to light the fire of fascination in the eyes of his students.

Now Vincent Scully is a Yale legend. Even up to his retirement at the age of seventy, his courses continued to be standing room only. I learned to appreciate both history and art—and do to this day. Because of one man. Because of his energy, enthusiasm, and excitement. Because he *communicated.*

The Two-Year-Old Speaks

Who are the best communicators in the world? Teachers? Actors? Politicians? Network news anchors? Stand-up comics?

No! Two-year-olds!

That's right, two-year-olds—those little Gerber-fed, Pampers-clad toddlers who have just been introduced to the power of speech are the *best* communicators in the world! Why? Because they have not been socialized yet. They have no inhibitions. They have just added the artillery of *words* to their arsenal of unrestrained energy. They don't care what anyone thinks of them, so they will shout, gesticulate, tug at you, make faces, cry, rant, and rave in order to get their message across! It's not that they are necessarily the most articulate—far from it. But they very often are the most persuasive.

Good persuasive communication is driven by energy. In the previous chapter, we saw that our personal energy is most forcefully conveyed through such visual components of communication as gestures and facial expressions. Those of us who are born with high levels of communicative energy—a naturally expressive face and voice or the gift of humor, movement, or untrammeled gesturing—have a natural advantage in reaching the listener's First Brain. But whether we are high- or low-energy communicators by nature, we can *all* become more aware of our energy levels—and we can all learn to increase our energy output.

UNLOCKING YOUR ENERGY

As communicators, we can learn (or relearn) a lot from two-year-olds. We can begin to shed some of the uptight, inhibited, self-limiting habits we have acquired over the years. The secret that Robert Kennedy had, that your favorite teacher had, that every two-year-old has, is essential and profound yet so simple to grasp: To unlock the communication process and get our point across, we must unlock our inner energy.

There's nothing mystical or magical about unlocking inner energy. It's not a matter of chanting a mantra or getting zapped by spiritual enlightenment. It's a simple matter of sharpening our skills and changing our behavior. And I do mean simple.

In the Decker training program, we divide personal impact into its component parts, then we focus on each part, one by one. We practice one skill, then the next, then the next. Before we know it, personal impact is in the process of positive change and on its way to becoming literally transformed!

At the beginning of this section, we listed the six ways to transform your personal impact. In Chapter 6, "The Eye Factor," we explored four of these six skills:

1. Eye Communication
2. Posture and Movement
3. Dress and Appearance
4. Gestures and the Smile

Those four skills are designed to transform our *visual* impact. The next two skills are designed to help us pack more *energy* into our message. They are:

5. Voice and Vocal Variety
6. Words and Nonwords (the Pause)

Now let's take a closer look at these two energy skills. You'll see how real people in real-life situations use them to be more effective communicators—and you'll see how easy it is for you to put the Energy Factor into your communication.

5. Voice and Vocal Variety

The Devil hath not, in all his quiver's choice, / An arrow for the heart like a sweet voice.
—Lord Byron

Your voice is the vehicle of your message. Learn to drive that vehicle like a Lamborghini. Push it, open it up, and, as my sixteen-year-old tells me, "Floor it!" Transmit the energy you have inside you through the vehicle of your voice!

Indeed, the voice is such an expressive instrument, and the First Brain of our listeners is so finely attuned to the signals carried in the voice, that a single word you speak can reveal volumes of information about you. Skeptical? Call a friend or family member on the phone and listen as they say, "Hello." Chances are you can tell that person's precise mood by the tone in which that one word is spoken.

What kind of voice do you have? Have you ever listened to your own voice on a tape? Did you like what you heard—or did you think, *That doesn't sound like me?*

Most people are surprised when they hear themselves on tape, and are absolutely convinced that the tape recorder has distorted their "true" voice. The fact is, the voice on the tape is much closer to what others actually hear than the voice we ourselves hear as we speak. So to hear ourselves as others hear us, we have to record ourselves—on the phone, in a meeting, or just in casual conversation—and listen carefully to the playback. It's the only way we can truly become aware of how much or how little energy we transmit when we speak.

EXAMPLES

- These days, few people recall how George H. W. Bush sounded when he was a candidate in the Republican primaries, running against another fellow named Reagan. Back then, one of the biggest complaints people had about George Bush was not his views but his voice, often described as high-pitched, reedy, and whiny. Critics cruelly dubbed him "The Wimp."

  Eight years later, Bush was again running for president. But this time he had been coached by Roger Ailes, the political media advisor to several Republican presidents and senators, including Reagan himself. One of the dramatic changes Ailes helped Bush make was to bring his voice down into a deeper, more authoritative range. In interviews, on the stump, and in the clinches of the Bush-Dukakis debates,

Bush's voice had just the right tone of strength and sincerity. The rest is—quite literally—history.

- Sensational accounts of steamy illicit sex guaranteed that videotape from Pamela Smart's murder trial would be carried on all the TV networks. At the end of the trial, she was convicted of conspiring to kill her husband. Because of her muted, monotonous voice and aloof composure, observers of the trial called her "The Ice Princess."

   After the trial, radio call-in shows buzzed with opinions about the convicted murderess. This remark by one caller was typical: "You could tell she was guilty by the way she talked. Flat, no emotion. If she was innocent of the accusations against her, you would have heard some emotion in her voice." The jury, of course, had a lot more evidence to go on than a First-Brain impression of the defendant's voice—but it's clear that her stony demeanor and toneless voice did little to help her case.

- A well-known corporate CEO was invited to give the dedication speech for a new building in a major city. A thousand people gathered for the event. After being introduced, he stepped up to the lectern and began reading his speech out of a manuscript his speechwriter had prepared. His voice was a deadly monotone. But deadlier still was the fact that page ten of the manuscript had been copied twice. Without even noticing, he read it twice. No one else noticed either, because no one else was listening. Actually, many had already left by the time he got to page ten.

- Jennifer Morales, a graduate student at Stanford University, was asked to give a talk to a community group on the life of John Steinbeck. She asked her English Lit professor to come to her talk, then evaluate her performance. The prof obliged, making himself comfortable in the center seat in the very front row.

   Throughout her talk, Jennifer stood glued to her lectern, speaking in a voice that would have left a perfectly flat trace on an oscilloscope. Within the first five minutes, the professor was quietly snoring way. Afterward, Jennifer indignantly confronted her professor. "You know I wanted your opinion of my speech," she said. "How could you go to sleep like that?" He simply replied, "My dear, sleep is an opinion."

The "reel" voice

It is often a shock to hear our voice on tape. It sounds different to our ear because the voice on the tape (and the voice others hear) is conducted by airwaves. The voice we hear when we speak is conducted through the bones in our head. If you want to know what others hear when they listen to you speak, you *must* listen to yourself on audiotape. That is where you will discover the strengths and weaknesses in your vocal quality and variety. And once you really *hear* your voice you'll be able to *change* your voice.

THE BASIC RULES

Make your voice naturally authoritative. If you discover you have a high, nasal-sounding voice, you can work on bringing it down into a lower register. One of the more valuable exercises that follows is the "King Kong" exercise, which will deepen your voice and give it flexibility. All it takes is practice—just a few minutes each day.

Is a rich, resonant voice really all that important? Have you ever heard such expressions as "listen to the voice of experience" or "that's the voice of authority"? Have you ever seen a movie or a TV show in which the voice of God was heard? Did that voice sound more like Orson Welles or Pee Wee Herman? (There's a reason Charlton Heston always plays Moses-like figures.) Clearly, people associate a rich, well-projected voice with authority and competence.

Put your voice on a roller coaster. Does your voice have a pleasing dynamic range? Does it rise and fall with the meaning of your words? Does it express emotion? Does it emphasize and underscore your message? Or do you speak in a monotone? Most of us do. To cure a monotonous voice, visualize your voice as a roller coaster: Lift it over the summit, then let it plummet. This mental exercise forces you to be aware of the dynamic range of your voice and puts you in the habit of extending that range by adding variety to your voice.

Be aware of your telephone voice. Professor Albert Mehrabian's research (Chapter 6) shows that your voice—the intonation, resonance, or auditory delivery of your message—counts for as much as (are you ready for this?) *84 percent* of your emotional impact and believability when people can't see you—such as when you're talking on the phone!

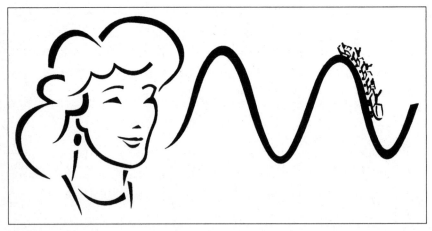

Ride the roller coaster

Does your telephone voice differ from your speaking voice? If so, why? Are you more expressive and energetic on the phone? How can you become more expressive and energetic in face-to-face situations? The exercises that follow will get you there.

Put your real feelings into your voice. Does the tone of your voice send out a different message than your words? Do you ever say, "It's good to talk to you," or, "I'm really excited to be here," in a flat, emotionless voice? Do you know how to put a smile into your voice?

That one is simple—just smile, and then talk. Try it when you practice with a tape recorder. Notice the difference? Be conscious of the emotional signals your voice sends. If you feel happy, excited, and enthusiastic, *let your voice show it.*

SOME BASIC EXERCISES

The voice has four basic components: *relaxation, breathing, projection,* and *resonance.* All of these components work together to make your voice uniquely your own. Each of these components can be altered and strengthened to allow your inner energy to come through when you speak. Here are some exercises to help you develop a more dynamic, authoritative voice.

Tone and relax. This set of tone and relax exercises is especially valuable just prior to giving a presentation. Find a place where you won't be disturbed—backstage, in the restroom, behind a potted plant. Then physically prepare yourself to communicate. Here's how:

- **Your Head and Neck.** Relax your jaw and let your mouth hang slightly open. Gently allow your head to settle so that your chin rests on your chest. Raise your head. Then let your head drop gently to your right shoulder. Raise it. Drop it gently to your left shoulder. Raise it.

  Now roll your head two times to the right. Then roll your head two times to the left.

  Monitor your breathing as you do these exercises. Breathe deeply from the diaphragm, but easily. The goal is to relax. Don't hold your breath. Keep your jaw loose, your mouth slightly open.

- **Your Shoulders.** Hands relaxed at your sides. Now . . . make two fists! Clench them. And with your fists still clenched, lift your shoulders all the way to your ears! . . . Okay, then, just get them as close to your ears as you can. Keep trying. Then stop.

  Drop your shoulders. Unclench your fists suddenly—shoot those fingers *out!* Sigh (let yourself hear it) as you exhale.

- **Your Face.** For reasons that will become obvious, we call this exercise "The Prune."

  First, make a tiny face. Try to push all your facial features in toward your nose. Pucker your lips. Squint your eyes. Scrunch your face muscles. Be a prune! Then . . . *go w-i-d-e! Surprise* your face! Open it as *wide* as you can!

  Now make another prune face! Then try to move your entire face—puckered lips, squinty eyes, and all—all the way to the right. Now move it all the way to the left.

  Then make that wide-open, surprised face again. Repeat the process several times.

- **Your Lips.** We call this "The Motorboat"—again for obvious reasons. Take a deep breath. Stick your lips out. Now force air through your puckered lips so that they vibrate and make a rolling *b-r-r-r-r-r* sound. Those vibrations help to relax your lips and prepare them for speaking.

Breathe from the diaphragm. Good vocal expression demands good breathing. This exercise will enable you to put real power into your voice.

Place your hands on your lower rib cage and inhale deeply through your nose, mouth closed. Your shoulders should remain still. Feel that expansion in your rib cage? That's caused by the contraction, or relaxation, of your diaphragm muscle.

Now exhale *slooooooowly* through your slightly open mouth. Feel the contraction of your rib cage? That's caused by the diaphragm muscle expanding, rising, and expelling the air from your lungs.

Do it again. And again. Keep practicing and experiencing that sensation of deep diaphragmatic breathing until it becomes effortless.

Now repeat the exercise with one hand on the front of your abdomen. When you breathe in, your abdomen should expand, shoving your hand away. The abdominal area of your body should fill up more fully than your chest. If not, then you are not inhaling deeply enough for the diaphragm to do its job.

Keep practicing. Make deep, diaphragmatic breathing a natural part of your daily "communications calisthenics." When you practice this exercise, you should feel a sensation of being relaxed, yet full of energy.

Do the "King Kong." This is great to relax your vocal chords before a speech—and to lower your voice. Let your mouth drop open. Inhale deeply through your nose—a deep breath from the diaphragm.

Now exhale. And as you exhale, say or sing the words "King Kong, Ding Dong, Bing Bong," in an up-and-down, singsong fashion. Start at a medium pitch and lower the tone, word by word, toward the deepest range of your voice. Let the words drop in tone like stones falling down a hilly mountainside into the valley below. Make that last "Bong" into a three-syllable word, and drop it in steps to the bottom of your range.

Gently, now! Don't strain your throat muscles reaching for that basso profundo! Again, the goal is to relax your voice so that it can find a deeper register.

As you exhale, relax your jaw. Let your mouth and throat open wide and easily, just like yawning. But gently, gently.

Repeat this several times. If you do this regularly (daily) you can permanently lower your voice. It's much like daily weight lifting—as long as you keep it up you will get the desired result: increased strength in the muscles that control your vocal cords. But stop, and the muscle turns to flab.

Learn to project your voice. Say a test sentence in your normal conversational voice. Then inhale through your nose—a deep breath from the diaphragm.

The "King Kong"

Now exhale, saying that same test sentence as you breathe out, and mentally *push* your voice out beyond the last row of an imaginary audience. Don't push the sound from your throat. Propel it from your stomach and diaphragm. Make your diaphragm support your voice.

Practice varying your pitch. Say various test sentences in a lilting, singsong, up-and-down fashion. Use poems or songs for your test sentences. Practice pumping feeling and conviction into your words as you say them. Let your voice be like a roller coaster.

Practice varying your pace. Try varying the speed of your delivery. Practice using a long pause. Record yourself with a tape recorder, phone answering machine, or camcorder. For material, read a passage from a book or a newspaper article. Read it with expression and conviction.

Use voice mail. Many of us now have access to voice mail systems in our companies. Voice mail is growing fast in the home market too, so most will be able to use it now, or soon, in a new way—to practice communication skills. Use it as a feedback tool. Send yourself a copy of a real message you are sending to a colleague or friend, and listen to the sound of your voice. Do it daily at first.

THE BENEFITS OF GOOD VOICE AND VOCAL VARIETY

- You are more effective on the telephone.
- You can convey emotions when you have a flexible voice.
- You are attractive to the ear.
- You have the capability to emphasize certain points and ideas with vocal energy and variation.
- You are First-Brain-friendly.

Remember: The world of business is a world of lower (resonant) voices. Join up, and project authority, vocal variety, and energy. Practice makes permanent!

6. Words and Nonwords(the Pause)

Another good way to put the Energy Factor in our communication is through our use of *words*. And a good way to drain the Energy Factor *out* of communication is through our use of *nonwords*. Let's take them one at a time. First let's discover how to energize and ignite our message through the use of . . .

Words

> Perhaps of all the creations of man, language is the most astonishing.
>
> Lytton Strachey

Mark Twain once said, "The difference between the right word and *almost* the right word is the difference between lightning and a lightning-bug." To put the energy of *lightning* in our message, we have to select the right words for the right situations. A rich, varied vocabulary and the ability to use it appropriately can spell the difference between "good enough" and *"great!"*

EXAMPLES

- In the wrong hands, language is lethal. And no form of language is more deadly than jargon. It can kill a conversation—instantly—as in this case:

    Overheard at a cocktail party:

    I've been a systems programmer on DECs, OS/2s, and VM/ CPs for six years, and I swear QMS has the friendliest command-line-oriented user interface in the field. It comes with the whole toolkit bundled in—editor, sort, text search, the whole whiz-bang! And the kernel interface supports every processing paradigm in the book—stop, suspend, wait, even hibernate. Of course, it has one humongous drawback. I mean, who wants to fork over a cool ten K for the same basic compiler you can get for five bills on your MS-DOS machine?

- "A word fitly spoken," says Proverbs 25:11, "is like apples of gold in pictures of silver." With just a little bit of effort every day, you too can make apples of gold every time you speak.

Jargon

THE BASIC RULES

Build your vocabulary. The English language is a powerful tool, loaded with extra attachments and gadgets called "synonyms." Because of the wealth of synonyms in our language, we can take a single thought and express it in virtually hundreds of ways. With a well-stocked vocabulary at our disposal, we can speak with precision, with subtle shades of meaning, with evocative imagery, and most of all with *energy.*

Does this mean we need to know a lot of "big words"? I beg to contravene that assertion. But we should have at our disposal the power to say "meticulous" instead of "careful," "conundrum" instead of "riddle," "pivotal" instead of "crucial," "endow" instead of "give," "disciple" instead of "follower," "rebuff" instead of "refuse," and "ad infinitum" (or even "ad nauseum") instead of "and so on and so forth."

It's easy to stretch your vocabulary. Just try to use one new word a day. If you come across a new word while you're reading a book or a magazine, jot it down, look it up in a dictionary, start using it in conversation, make it your own. Don't use words to show off, but continually be on the lookout for new words that can help you communicate in the clearest, most colorful, most interesting way for every situation.

Paint word pictures. Language can do a lot more for our message than merely give us multiple ways of expressing an idea. Language can pack the Energy Factor into our communication by enabling us to paint intense, colorful word pictures. We can lend the energy of both *motion and emotion* to our speech by the use of metaphors and vivid expressions.

With a little imaginative language, the night sky becomes a "sparkling cosmic ocean." An F-16 fighter-bomber becomes a "screaming bird of prey." A freeway at night becomes "a river of glowing red coals." The stock market didn't just rise, it "broke the price barrier." The politician didn't just evade the question, he "bobbed, weaved, and juked."

These are not "big words" used to impress other people with how smart we are. They are, for the most part, fairly simple words, but put together in ways that create memorable, exciting images, and those images make vivid impressions on the First Brain of our listener. Our goal is not to impress, but *to make an impression.* Rich and varied language can be one of the best tools at our command for getting our point across with energy and impact.

Beware of jargon. If you are in a profession that uses a lot of jargon—careful! Jargon can be a convenient form of shorthand communication when educators talk to other educators, doctors talk to doctors, lawyers talk to lawyers, computer programmers talk to computer programmers, and so on. But when you are moving in circles outside your professional field, you have to speak English again!

Like the fellow talking about "OS/2s," "kernel interfaces," and "processing paradigms" at the cocktail party, jargon addicts don't communicate. They just turn people off. Jargon addicts convey the impression that they feel superior to their listeners. Those who have to endure the babble of acronyms and technical language soon slam their First Brains shut. Whatever the jargon-babbler says bounces uselessly off the closed doors of his listeners' minds.

Nonwords (the Pause)

The notes I handle no better than many pianists. But the pauses between the notes—ah, that is where the art resides!

Artur Schnabel

Everyone knows that language is made out of words. But did you know that language is also made out of nonwords? To communicate effectively, you must be aware of nonwords that obstruct your message. The most common nonwords are *uhh, ahh,* and *umm.* Others include such sounds and phrases as *so, well, you know, and, okay, like, sort of,* and similar nonsense noises we use to fill the empty spaces in our communication. As in "Well . . . uhhh . . . my name is Joe Smith . . . uhhh, annnnnnnd I'm here to sort of talk about Effective Communicating: . . . umm . . . the Key to, uh, Success. And . . . uhhh . . . I want to thank you all for being here . . . soooo . . . umm, let's get started, okay?"

Nonwords bleed the Energy Factor right out of your message. They make you appear hesitant, uncertain, incompetent. The listener's First Brain is put on guard against your message. Your listener wonders— usually at a preconscious but very real level—*If this speaker isn't confident about his or her message, why should I believe it?*

EXAMPLE

- Joyce is an account exec with a large advertising agency in Southern California. Her job is to persuade corporate clients to spend money with her firm so that their companies can sell their products and services more effectively. Joyce is good at what she does. She has a pleasant, authoritative voice and a confident presence. But she has an unfortunate habit of ending many of her sentences with "Okay?" She continually seems to be asking for agreement—a habit that undermines her air of confidence and the effectiveness of her communication.

Let's face it: Most of us are *addicted* to using nonwords that choke our energy level and retard the effectiveness of our communication. In short, we are "uhhh-dicted." But there is a way out with the help of some simple behavior modification techniques.

Nonwords

THE BASIC RULES

Find your level of nonwords. Years before I knew very much about communicating, I recorded a speech I gave and was *shocked* to hear thirty-five nonwords in the first two minutes! I can't overemphasize the power of feedback to uncover your communicating weaknesses so you can deal with them. Listen to yourself on tape. Count the nonwords you use. You will probably wince a lot as you listen—but you'll also become more aware. That awareness will help you control the nonword habit.

Replace your nonwords with something more powerful. You're probably thinking, *But what if I can't live without my nonwords? What happens if there's a big silent* gap *in my sentence while I'm thinking of the next phrase? Don't I need to fill those gaps with some sort of sound?* No. You fill those gaps with something *infinitely* more powerful than meaningless sounds. You fill those gaps with something that gives energy and drama to your message: the Pause.

Use the "power of the Pause." Did you know that the Pause can be one of your most dynamic communicating tools? You can pause for as long as three or four seconds, right in the middle of a sentence, and it will not only seem perfectly natural to your listener, it will give extra punch to your message.

The problem with pausing is that most of us have never tried it. We are afraid of silence in our communication. We're not used to pausing, so we rush to fill the silence with inane and meaningless sound—sound that dampens our Energy Factor and blunts the point of our message.

Let me suggest an experiment. The next time you have a conversation with a close friend, pay attention to your nonwords and replace them with a pause. Instead of saying "uhhh" or "ummm," just wait three or four seconds while you gather your thoughts for the next phrase or sentence. Sure, it'll *seem* like twenty seconds in your own mind, but your friend won't even notice. In fact, a beat or two of silence now and

The Pause

then actually heightens the intensity and the energy of your message, while helping to hold the interest of your listener.

SOME BASIC EXERCISES

Exercises in *pausing* will probably have the second biggest and most immediate payoff in your communications effectiveness. (Exercises in eye communication will be number one.) You will not only get rid of nonwords, but in gaining the power of the Pause, you gain thinking time and can add drama to your impact.

Record yourself. Use video or audio taping regularly to practice leaving pauses, and to sensitize yourself to your nonword patterns. It won't take long for you to sharpen your ear to those irritants. In fact, you'll soon begin catching yourself *before* the nonword comes out of your mouth, and you'll replace it with a pause. Being conscious of nonwords is the first step to eliminating them.

Use voice mail. Use your voice mail system as a feedback tool. Send yourself a copy of a real message you are sending to a colleague or friend, and listen to your pauses, or nonwords. Do it daily at first.

Practice with a buddy. Have a friend listen while you give an impromptu talk. Ask him or her to instantly say your name every time you use a nonword. For some of us, the nonword habit is so ingrained that we will not even notice it when it is pointed out to us. We may even feel picked on unfairly: "I did *not* say 'uhh.'" It helps to work with a friend who is trying to get rid of his or her own nonword habit so you can trade off.

Practice the Pause. When you feel tempted to lapse into a nonword, just *pause.* Let the Pause hover lightly in the air—for three, four, five, six seconds, or even more—while you gather your thoughts for the next sentence. Push your pauses to the limit. Then get feedback on your pauses: Did they seem forced or natural? Did they heighten the drama of your message and grab your listeners' attention? Remember the disparity that you will feel. It is valuable to get this experience of disparity many times over. You'll be surprised to discover how natural and confident you sound when you have learned the power of the Pause.

THE BENEFITS OF GOOD WORDS AND NO NONWORDS

- You are memorable in your language.
- You appear confident and intelligent.
- You can use the Pause for dramatic emphasis.
- You no longer belong to the great mass of nonword irritators.
- You become more First-Brain-friendly.

Remember: Use colorful, jargonless language, and replace nonwords with a good three-second pause.

Unleashing the Energy Within

People like and trust the person who puts all of his or her conviction into motion, expression, vocal variety, and memorable language. People respond warmly to the speaker who displays humanity and humor. The Energy Factor is right there inside you, waiting to be unleashed.

All the communicative energy you need, you already have. Learn to release and direct the Energy Factor—then watch it ignite your communication, inspire your listeners, and change the direction of your life.

Part IV

Mastering Your First Brain

U p to this point we have been talking about what you can do to affect and reach the First Brain of your listener. Not your audience. Your *listener*. Remember, every person within the sound of your voice is a *singular* person, whether you are communicating one-on-one or to a packed house. The first seven chapters of this book have been focused on reaching the First Brain of your listener.

Now, in Part IV, it's time to look inward, to the First Brain that powers *your own* personality. Through the next two chapters, we will examine what you can do to better *control* and *utilize* the driving force of your own First Brain. We will discover how your *First* Brain—the unreasoning, feeling part of your mind—can be brought under the conscious control of your thinking, reasoning, decision-making *New* Brain.

Until now, we have seen the First Brain as passive, an important but helpless gate in the listener's mind that opens and closes according to the signals and cues the speaker sends forth. But at this point we will explore the enormous active power of your own First Brain to transform your life for the better or, if poorly understood and directed, to strangle your future.

The two chapters of Part IV are:

- **Chapter 8: First-Brain Fear.** This is *the* crucial issue for many of us: *the fear of public speaking.* In this chapter we will discover why we feel the way we do about speaking, what the fight-or-flight response is, and why it wields such enormous power.

- **Chapter 9: First Brain Under Control.** How to *conquer* our First-Brain fear of speaking is the important subject of this chapter. And how to harness the energy of our own First Brain to make us more effective and persuasive.

CHAPTER 8

First-Brain Fear

Do the thing you fear, and the death of fear is certain.

Ralph Waldo Emerson

Fear on the Run

Speaking is what I do, and I do it all the time. I speak to large audiences. I speak in small workshop and seminar settings. I speak on TV. Public speaking holds no terror for me anymore—but it used to. Much more than I like to admit. In fact, it wasn't too long ago that I first discovered how to overcome the fear of public speaking.

It was in 1981—a little over a year after I founded Decker Communications. I had accepted an invitation to be the main presenter at a regional meeting of ASTD—the American Society for Training and Development. After I accepted, the first thing I thought was, *Why did I get into this business anyway?*

In those days, when my knees were in better shape, I used to exercise many days by running up and down the hills of San Francisco. Right on my running path was the Holiday Inn on Van Ness Avenue—the site of the forthcoming ASTD meeting. I have vivid memories of those morning runs, sucking in that crisp Pacific air as I chugged to the crest of a hill, my Nikes snick-snickering on the pavement—and then I would see . . . *it.*

By *it* I mean the Holiday Inn. I shouldn't make it sound so horrible, because it's a nice enough building, really. But to me it was as ominous and forbidding as the old house on the hill above the Bates Motel in *Psycho*. Here it was, a full *six months* before I was to give that speech, and the mere sight of the Holiday Inn made my blood congeal and my stomach turn somersaults. And this didn't happen just one or two times. It happened *every time* I passed that building.

Sure, it was an important speech. After all, this was the first major exposure of my fledgling company before many potential buyers of my services. A lot was riding on it.

But I had to wonder why I was even in the communications business if I had such an intense fear of public speaking. It was like the president of Bank of America keeping his money in a mattress, or the president of McDonald's being a vegetarian, or the president of General Motors owning a Kia, or the president of Philip Morris not smoking. I realized that if I couldn't conquer my fear of public speaking, I was a fraud and didn't deserve to be in the business.

I tried to talk myself out of my fear. I tried to psyche myself up. But as the day of the speech grew closer, my fear only increased.

Then the day came. Shark music thundered in my head, as the theme from *Jaws* grew louder and louder: "Dum-dum. Dum-dum. Dum-dum. Dum-dum!" As I stepped up to speak, I was one big jangling, terrified nerve. I faced the audience. I opened my mouth. And I spoke.

My presentation was videotaped, and I got to see the videotape the next day. I was utterly amazed. I knew of the disparity phenomenon—heck, I even taught it—but it was profound to experience it so personally. You couldn't tell how nervous I was! It didn't show in the slightest! What an astounding difference between the way I felt and the way I looked.

Not only that, I wasn't bad. I was even persuasive—so persuasive that I convinced a skeptic. Fred Verhey was in the audience. I didn't know him then. He was a trainer for a restaurant chain at the time, and was impressed enough to come and do the Decker Program. Within six months we hired Fred, and he became a vice president in our company. He's a great speaker, too. That terror-drenched speech was my first connection with Fred.

Public speaking used to spook, scare, rattle, and unnerve me—but no longer. I learned how to disarm the fear of public speaking. I knew I had to if I was going to stay in this business. The ASTD speech in 1981 was the spark that sent me on a search for answers and solutions to this fear.

I have learned those answers and found those solutions. Today I practice what I preach. I've gone through the confidence-building process that I hope you embark on—and in the coming pages I'm going to tell you exactly how to get there yourself.

Sure, I still have an emotional reaction before a speaking "performance." But now it's excitement and exhilaration, not raw fear. It's the kind of reaction a sprinter feels as he steps into the starting blocks—the healthy edge of tension that powers a Class A performance.

The fear of speaking is a First-Brain fear. It's irrational—and knowing it's irrational doesn't help one bit. But knowing *where* this irrational fear comes from, *how* it affects you, and how you can *control* it helps immensely.

By the end of these next two chapters, you'll know everything you need to know to send fear on the run.

The Fear of Speaking

The following chart of people's greatest fears is best known from *The Book of Lists* but it was originally researched some years ago in a survey by *The Sunday Times* of London.[1] And I can affirm that the facts are true from my own experience with Decker Communications. We have trained over two hundred thousand people, and I can assure you that, almost without exception, everyone who comes through our programs can testify to the truth of this research.

But why? Why should the fear of speaking loom larger than any other threat in our lives? Why would we literally rather *die* than get up before an audience and communicate? It's totally irrational—and you

Greatest Fears

	%
1. Speaking	41
2. Heights	32
3. Insects & bugs	22
4. Financial	22
5. Deep water	22
6. Sickness	19
7. Death	19

and I both know it. And we also know that the fear of communicating limits our effectiveness and hinders our careers and our relationships.

Irrational though it may be, the fear is *real.* It has real causes—and fortunately, it has real solutions.

The fear of public speaking has its genesis in the way our First Brain works.

THE SOURCE OF FEAR

The fear of public speaking is actually many fears bundled together. Broken into its component parts, the fear of public speaking—often called "performance anxiety"—becomes easier to understand and to overcome. The first thing to understand about this anxiety is that it is actually the fear of making ourselves vulnerable before others (exposure). Added to this is the fear of failure (ridicule). These component fears, which become exaggerated to wildly unrealistic proportions in our minds, have the power to stimulate genuine mortal dread within us at the prospect of speaking in public.

The reason this fear can be so overpowering and paralyzing is that it is First-Brain fear—unreasoning, preconscious animal fear, related to our instincts for survival. Remember that the First Brain does not reason or analyze. It reacts emotionally. It registers needs, and it responds to threats of danger, and it controls certain physiological responses as part of the body's autonomic and sympathetic nervous system. When our New Brain analyzes a situation (such as speaking before an audience) as a threat, it sends many stimuli—siren alarms of danger—to our First Brain. The First Brain responds with naked animal fear and physiological responses that are not under our conscious control.

Our palms sweat. Our hearts palpitate. Our throats constrict. Blood pressure increases. Adrenaline surges.

That's the reaction I experienced while running past the Holiday Inn on Van Ness Avenue. It was a First-Brain reaction. That's why I couldn't control the way I felt, even six months before the day of the speech. I didn't know then what I know now.

You can't reason with your First Brain. You can't control its responses. But there is a way to bring First-Brain fear under control. It all takes place in your New Brain, the thinking and reasoning part of your brain. You control First-Brain fear by modifying the attitude in your New Brain that triggers the fear.

FIGHT OR FLIGHT

The basis of First-Brain fear is a psychological and behavioral principle called the "fight-or-flight response." It's a survival mechanism that developed in very primitive forms of life and that has grown more powerful and elaborate in more complex forms of life, such as you and me.

An example of this primitive survival mechanism is the way freshwater snails jerk into their shells when touched by a predator, or the way baby chicks instinctively crouch and freeze in response to an alarm call by the mother hen. In reptiles and lower mammals, this survival mechanism includes the ability to fight and attack a predator alongside the ability to run and hide.

Your First Brain and mine are like computers with very basic programming written into their circuits. The program is called "fight or flight." When faced with a perceived threat (whether that threat is objectively real or not), the primitive computer of the First Brain analyzes the situation in terms of a very simple decision: "Should I flee and hide—or should I stand and fight?"

All the First Brain cares about is survival. The fight-or-flight response is one of the survival programs etched in the hardwired circuitry of your First Brain.

There was a time, millennia ago, when the fight-or-flight response served our prehistoric ancestors quite well. If you've ever seen pictures of prehistoric predators, you know there were times that our predecessors needed to make some lightning-fast, life-or-death decisions. There wasn't time for analysis. Whether the choice was to fight or flee, they literally had to move it or lose it.

So if Mr. or Mrs. Australopithecus happened to be on the way to the watering hole when a saber-toothed tiger leaped out from the underbrush, he or she wouldn't have to think. Everything would take place at a preconscious, First-Brain level—in virtually a reflex action. Blood would rush to the muscles of Mr. or Mrs. A's body, preparing it to run. Glycogen would be changed to glucose for energy. Adrenaline would move the mind to think more quickly. A flush of perspiration would occur instantly and automatically to cool the body, now ready and heated for action.

Of course, this primitive individual is not completely at the mercy of these reflex responses. If the tiger in question has teeth as long as your forearm and weighs four hundred pounds, there is only one choice: Get out of here! But if Mr. or Mrs. A is a big-boned individual armed with a stout club and Mr. Tiger is a cat of modest size and ferocity, our prehistoric ancestor may be confident enough to whoop the tar out of that kitty.

Now, my suspicion is that you don't encounter too many saber-toothed tigers on the way to the office water cooler. But the physiological reactions that Mr. or Mrs. A experienced in the presence of the saber-toothed tiger are probably very familiar to you. Perhaps you experienced those sensations one time when you were confronted by a mugger. Or when a speeding car came at you while you were in the crosswalk. Or when you stood in front of an audience, about to give a speech.

Strange, isn't it, that a natural survival response that served our ancestors so well—and that *still* serves us well in dangerous situations—can also hurt us, limit our effectiveness, and mess up our performance at those times when we desperately want to do our best. But it's true.

So what can we do? We can teach our thinking, reasoning New Brains to stop shouting "Danger!" at our First Brains. We can teach our New Brains the difference between real and imagined threats.

A FRIENDLY EXPERIMENT

It was one of those perfect summer evenings—a dinner party at our home with three other couples. The sun had just set as we finished dinner and went for the view in the living room. From the picture window of our hillside house, we could see the headlights prowling the valley below. Over the mountains, stars were just peeking through the deepening twilight.

"Just perfect," said Emily, one of our guests. She was looking out the window at the gathering dusk, cradling a tulip glass of cabernet.

I didn't know Emily well. I knew she was a very successful sales executive for a large company in the Bay Area. I could tell from talking to her that she was a confident person. She exuded poise and competence, and she was a good conversationalist.

"Bert," she said, "I know you have a communications company of some kind, but I don't understand what kind of communications you're involved with. Do you work with telecommunications? Computer networks? Phone systems?"

"I work with people."

"Well, you could say we *all* work with people, but—"

"No, I mean I really work with *people*," I said. "I help people communicate more effectively, giving speeches or sales presentations, or communicating one-on-one. I teach people how to get their message across more persuasively, and how to overcome the fear of public speaking."

"Fear of public speaking?" she said. I detected a glint of condescension in her smile and in her tone. Maybe it was always there—but I just now recognized it. "Are there really that many people who are afraid of something as simple as giving a talk in front of an audience?"

"It's the number one fear," I replied. "People are more afraid of speaking in public than they are of death." And I proceeded to tell her about the results of the *Sunday Times* of London survey.

"You're joking!"

"I'm not."

"That's too bad. I've never felt that way," she said. And then went on to talk effusively and enthusiastically about a new project she had just launched for her company. While she talked for the next few minutes, the wheels in my mind were turning.

"Emily," I said during a pause in the conversation, "would you try an experiment?"

She glanced at me from the corners of her eyes, intrigued but wary. "What do you have in mind?"

"Trust me," I said. "I think you'll find this very interesting. Maybe even educational."

"Okay," she said, even more wary than before. "What do I do?"

"Very simple. All you have to do is tell us the story you just told us. About the new project with your company. Tell it exactly as you did before, but with one little difference. This time, stand up while you speak."

"Sure," she said, relieved that the experiment turned out to be a piece of cake. She stood up and took a few steps back from the table, then began to speak. "As I was telling you—the, uh, project I—"

We all saw it. Although it wasn't exactly a hunted look that came into her eyes, it was no longer that cocksureness either. Her hands assumed the classic "fig-leaf" position—a sure sign of nervousness.

She didn't finish her first sentence before saying, "This is different! Standing up here with all of you looking at me like this, I don't feel I'm just chatting with friends anymore. I feel . . . *judged.*"

OUR MIND DOES IT TO US

What happened to Emily? What caused her to freeze up?

Just moments before, she had been talking effectively, excitedly, confidently as she described something in her life that she felt enthusiastic about. What changed? The room was the same. The listeners were the same. The message was the same. In fact, *nothing at all changed* except the fact that Emily was now "presenting" instead of just communicating with friends.

Her mind did it to her. Even though she was still among friends, she felt she was standing in the hot glare of the spotlight. She imagined her "audience" was gauging her "performance" with a critical eye. Even though nothing had changed, *everything* had changed in Emily's mind because *she felt she was being judged as she spoke.*

The conclusion that she was being judged came from her New Brain. Her New Brain sent a message to her First Brain: "Danger!" Now she not only felt she was performing, but she also felt threatened. The fight-or-flight response took over: Adrenaline, nervousness, and fear suddenly replaced her former excitement, enthusiasm, and confidence.

And communication ceased.

CHILDHOOD DISASTERS

Poor little Janny. She learned about hurt at a very early age. Her parents loved her and never abused her. But still she experienced some very deep hurts, and her First Brain still bears the scars.

Janny's older sister, Beth, had a cruel streak. She resented Janny from the day she was born, because baby Janny got all the attention and Beth got shoved aside. So, whenever her parents weren't looking, Beth took her resentment out on Janny in small ways. Inflicting pain. Inflicting humiliation. Name-calling. Telling Janny she was stupid or ugly or unloved or unwanted.

Once, when Janny was two years old and Beth was six, big sister punched little sister in the face to make her stop laughing. It split her lip—four stitches.

But one of the most emotionally devastating events in Janny's young life had nothing to do with the cruelty of her older sister. It happened at the church picnic when Janny was eight years old. The children were playing softball in the park next to the church.

Janny stood behind the chain-link backstop, awaiting her turn at bat. At the plate was eleven-year-old Jeff—the pastor's son and the object of Janny's infatuation. He had just taken a mighty swing and knocked the ball deep into left field.

Janny started to shout, "Great shot!" but in the split second before the words came out of her mouth, she tried to change it to "Great hit!" What came out of her mouth, what everyone at the church picnic heard, what her horrified parents could not ignore, were the shrill words "Great shit!" And at the top of her little lungs. That was not at all what she had meant to say. Suddenly all eyes were staring at her. Even Jeff looked over his shoulder in amazement as he ran to first base. He laughed. Janny burst into tears.

She never forgot the shame and embarrassment of inadvertently shouting an obscenity before a crowd of people. Never.

In her college speech course (which she took only because it was required), she painfully stammered her way to a C minus—nothing more than a sympathy grade. In her church and her job, she carefully avoided situations that might require her to speak.

The First-Brain fear that was hammered into her at an early age by a resentful sister and a traumatic childhood experience is with her to this day. Janny—or Janice, as she is now known—is thirty-eight years old and scared to death of public speaking.

There's nothing unusual about Janice's story. Her childhood was, on balance, no more unhappy or painful than that of most people. But her future is crippled by the First-Brain fear that she learned at a very early age.

Does Janny's story remind you of your own story? Could it be that your own First-Brain fear is rooted in things that happened to you in childhood? Could it be that the taunts and petty cruelties and abuses you suffered twenty or thirty or forty years ago are still hurting you,

NORMAN VINCENT PEALE ON SELF-ESTEEM

"I, once spoke in New Orleans at a convention of elementary school principals. There were nine thousand there and I got to visiting with a lot of them. One of the things we talked about was self-esteem. When a child is born he is born as a positive personality, but they said that by the time they get to the fourth or fifth grade, eighty to eighty-five percent of them have a low self-esteem. They are negative, and that low self-esteem tends to continue during their high school and their college careers, and on into their adult life. And I had never heard that before, so I interrogated all the teachers that I have spoken to in various states and nationally and they corroborated this. Low self-esteem is a major problem in today's world."

From a conversation with Dr. Norman Vincent Peale.[2]

still holding you back, still keeping you from achieving the grown-up goals of your life?

When our cerebral cortex—our New Brain—is just being imprinted and developed in early childhood, the First Brain is the driving force. We are extremely vulnerable to the pain of judgment and criticism. The cruel taunts of siblings and other children and the appraisal of stern parents are quickly and indelibly etched into the wet cement of a child's mind.

Patterns of insecurity, fear, self-doubt, and self-criticism are set, for most of us, at a very early age. These patterns emerge in our adulthood as a lack of confidence in situations where we are called upon to perform, to expose ourselves to the appraisal of our peers. Hence the term *performance anxiety.*

Think for a moment: What is it you are really afraid of when you contemplate speaking in public?

Is it judgment? Are you afraid of what other people will think of you? Are you afraid of embarrassment? Of failure? Of taking further crippling blows to your self-esteem?

All of these things sound pretty horrible. But now that we are adults, do we *really* have so much to fear from the judgment of other people?

The 95-Percent Solution

The deeper and more profound truth about our fear of being judged is that this fear is so terribly exaggerated and misplaced. The tragedy is that we needlessly limit ourselves by our fear, because we aren't faulted by others anywhere near as much or as often as we think we are.

Psychologists Abraham Maslow and Karen Horney both did extensive work on the development of self-esteem and self-worth in an individual. Maslow's "hierarchy of needs" theory leading to self-actualization is now classic, but I think Horney's work has perhaps an even stronger application. She found that when an individual actually attempts something—intellectually or physically, be it a memory verse, an athletic event, going for a promotion, or even a speech—the great majority of the time the individual will succeed. Yet when a person does not make the attempt, they have an impression of failure. The dramatic finding is that for most people their self-impression is one of failure more than success *because most of the time they do not make the attempt.*

I have tracked this with myself and others and found that about 95 percent of the time that we attempt to speak—to communicate—we succeed. The first time I realized that, I thought, *Wow! Ninety-five percent?* (Major league ballplayers are doing great if they are batting above .300.) But I've tested the thesis, I've done the experiment. My test has been anecdotal rather than scientific, to be sure, but I have verified Dr. Horney's theories. Looking objectively at my meetings, communications, and speeches over a set time period, I had to say I really *was* batting around .950, just as Dr. Horney indicated. That's pretty dramatic.

And the same is true of *you.* About 95 percent of the time, you're going to succeed at communicating. So why not play the odds? Every time you attempt a speech and feel the tug of self-doubt, tell yourself that this is going to be one of your "95-percent" performances. If, when it's all over, it turns out to be one of those rare "5-percent" duds, so be it. Accept it, learn from it, and move on.

Consider this: *Why should you jeopardize every performance for the sake of that 5 percent?* Yet that, unfortunately, is what most of us do.

You don't have to do that to yourself any longer. Here you have already acquired some insights that can help your New Brain quell the irrational fears of your First Brain. You know that your physical survival is not at stake when you stand up and communicate with others. You know that you have little if anything to fear from the judgment of others. You are batting .950, and that puts you in a class *beyond* the major leagues. In short, you are better than you think you are!

And the best is yet to come.

CHAPTER 9

First Brain Under Control

The Case of the Pounding Heart

My late wife, Deborah, was my partner in founding and operating Decker Communications. Deborah was a very articulate and engaging lady. When questioned, her responses not only exuded confidence but were also stamped with her own special sense of humor. Her wit and insight were always right on the mark, and audiences and interviewers were invariably charmed by her personality.

Just a few months after Deborah and I formed our training company, we were asked to appear on a TV panel show. The subject was "Fear of Speaking."

During the show, she fielded the first question with great poise and apparent ease. It was clear that her answer was very persuasive. As she spoke, I noticed her right hand cross her body and lightly touch the area just over her heart, then fall back onto her lap.

Later at home we were watching the videotape of the show. At the point where she began answering that tough question, I heard her murmur in astonishment, "You can't even tell how nervous I was!"

"Nervous?" I said. "You know, you said you were nervous, but I still don't believe you. It doesn't show at all."

"Wait," she replied. "Rewind the tape a little. . . ."

I did, and we looked at the TV screen. Her right hand moved up, touched the area over her heart, then fell back into her lap. "At that moment my heart was hammering so hard I thought it was going to burst out of my chest!" she said. "I put my hand over my heart to cover up the fluttering. I really thought it showed."

As Deborah sat beside me and described her jangled inner feelings, I studied that *other* Deborah on the video screen. She appeared as confident and charming as ever. Her answer was bright and penetrating, her manner completely controlled and self-assured. Where was all this mortal fear she said was going on inside? It certainly didn't show in any heart flutter. And it didn't show on her face, in her eyes, or in her voice.

Clearly the fight-or-flight response was ringing off the walls inside Deborah's First Brain—though she was the only one who knew. Ironically, while she was talking on TV about the fear of speaking, that fear was raging inside her like a five-alarm fire. Yet on the outside she was the picture of poise and confidence.

Since those early days at the founding of Decker Communications, I have made an intensive study of the fear of speaking, its causes and its cure. And the cure for this near-universal fear lies in learning to bring our First Brain under control.

The Life Force

The greatest 400-meter hurdler in history was Edwin Moses. He won the Olympic gold medal in 1976 with a record-setting time of *47.63* seconds—a time he trimmed to a new record of 47.02 seconds in 1983. From 1976 to 1987, he astounded the world with a string of 119 consecutive victories.

What was going on in the mind of this phenomenal athlete each time he crouched at the starting blocks? Was he worried about survival? About what people would think of his performance? No. Was he worried about winning? I doubt it, because in nearly every race he ran, Moses won by wide margins. After thirty, fifty, or a hundred consecutive wins, I would think he had confidence.

But was he nervous? I'm certain of it. Not because he was afraid of losing, but because he wasn't sure *how well* he was going to do! Would this be the day he broke his own record again? Maybe—with just a little extra competitive edge.

Edwin Moses was a champion because he used the adrenaline-charged fight-or-flight reflex of the First Brain. He channeled the physiological force of the First Brain to power his performance over the hurdles.

You can speak the way Edwin Moses jumped. Or at least make a grand stride in that direction. You can channel the awesome power of the First Brain that athletes use to give you that competitive edge every time you speak.

Your First Brain is an unbridled powerhouse of raw emotions, urges, and needs. It's the energy force that drives you—that powers your wants and desires, your sense of excitement and satisfaction, your feelings of joy and fear.

Picture the tremendous power of a 5,000-psi firehose. It's hooked up to the hydrant, water is roaring through it, but there's no one directing its force. It whipsaws like a wounded cobra, spewing a blast of water that knocks people off their feet and drenches everything within a hundred-foot radius. That's what the uncontrolled First Brain is like.

Now picture a firefighter confronting a five-story inferno. Alone, he is a pretty puny challenger against such a raging force. But put that 5,000-psi firehose in his grip and watch what happens! Now you have a powerfully effective force for good. That firefighter is like your New Brain—well trained, flexible, smart, with a fantastically potent tool at his command.

That's what the First Brain is like under the conscious control of the New Brain. The fight-or-flight response doesn't have to destroy us. We can command it. It is in our power. This is one of the things that separates human beings from other animals: our New Brain, and its capacity to rule the First Brain. All other animals—dogs, dolphins, lions, and even the primates such as chimps, gorillas, and orangutans—are essentially motivated by primitive First-Brain impulses. They have no conscious control over those impulses. You and I do. The smart thing is to learn how to effectively exercise that control.

Controlling the First Brain

Dynamic Tension

To some degree, we all exercise a measure of First-Brain control, but we all could do much better than we do.

Let's face it: Public speaking means speaking under pressure. Pressure and inner tension are involved whenever we speak in public because we are exposing ourselves to public appraisal. And speaking under pressure is the most important kind of communication we do. There's a lot on the line: reputation, personal satisfaction, fulfillment of others' expectations, and even career advancement.

It's the *pressure* aspect of public speaking that suggests a parallel between speaking and athletic performance. Because we have so much on the line, we want to have all the natural excitement, enthusiasm, and confidence at our disposal *working for us.* That's what athletes do: direct the pressure and tension they feel into the energy needed to power their best performance.

That's why you never want to get rid of your performance anxiety. In its proper balance, performance anxiety is essential to a great performance. Ethel Merman once said, "I know my lines, what's there to be nervous about?" I suspect Miss Merman was a bit disingenuous. A little nervousness—let's call it dynamic tension—translates into energy to

---

NO MAGIC PILL

"The first couple of words, it's like—I get an immediate case of dry mouth, and that makes it difficult to talk. You stumble over your words and then you even get more nervous, because you know you are messing up, and it's frustrating."

Michelle Felde was the star of a recent *20/20* program on the fear of speaking. ABC brought their camera crews into our video feedback training, and Michelle was one of our students. She worked for Ingres Corporation—a fast-growing software company—and was making a transition from computer support work to marketing management. She was taking the Decker Program to help prepare for her new role.

The *20/20* camera crews followed her through the program and a consulting session with Bob Figari, one of our senior trainers. Then they covered a real presentation she gave a month later to see how she did, and what became of her fear of speaking. So Michelle had to "perform" with not only the normal pressure of a video training program, but with the possibility of being seen by a national television audience on top of that. How did she do?

Brilliantly, which is why the producers used her for most of this *20/20* program. It was a thrill for us, too, to see the confidence that comes from video feedback training demonstrated on national television.

But the most telling piece of the program was in the last shot. From a closeup Michelle said, "Actually if they could just develop maybe a pill that you took, that took care of the sweaty palms and the adrenaline and all that, I mean that would be great."

But there is no pill, so the ABC interviewer asked why she subjected herself to this pressure.

"If I had stepped back and said, 'No, I couldn't do it,' it would have been real self-defeating. And so this was the chance to say 'Okay, you had this problem of fear, so let's go for it and what the heck, let's do it on national TV.'

"It's been good, yeah. It's been real good."

help us do our best. Obviously, there's a line between dynamic tension and fear, and it's a line we don't want to cross. But a mild case of "backstage jitters" can be an asset to a good performance.

Remember, we succeed at 95 percent of the tasks we attempt. So we know that we will almost certainly do well when we get up to speak—but sometimes we don't know *how* well. That little bit of surplus nervous energy can be the extra edge that sends our performance to unexpected heights!

The object is not to get rid of the butterflies but to get the butterflies to fly in formation.

When the Angels Descend

Patricia Fripp is one of the top professional speakers in the United States and Great Britain. She is a petite, winsome engine of communicative energy with a charming English accent. She's a pro, and she always knows she'll be good. She just never knows exactly *how* good.

Patricia's brother is Robert Fripp, one of the most popular guitarists in England. Patricia says the quote she often uses about her speeches originally came from Robert talking about his concert performances: "I know I'll always be good, but I never know whether the angels will descend."

I know what they mean—and you should too. We have confidence to know we will be effective, we will be good—but there will be those times when we will be *great*. You can never predict when those times will come, when "the angels will descend." But those times *will* come—and when those angels descend, they'll be riding on lightning bolts of First-Brain energy.

You and I can have the same winning confidence of Robert Fripp, of Patricia Fripp—and of an athlete like Edwin Moses. Every time the starting pistol fired, Moses came out of the blocks knowing he would be good—but never knowing if he was going to soar over those hurdles in 47.63 seconds, 47.02 seconds, or maybe (if a whole heavenly band of angels came down) 47 flat. He never knew and neither do we.

But the possibility is always there. *That's* the possibility that should ignite our First Brain, not the slim chance of failure: the thought that maybe, just maybe, tonight is the night we "push the envelope," the night our energy propels us beyond what we thought we could accomplish.

It can happen to you. It *will* happen to you—if you plug into the power of your First Brain, and learn to direct its power in the direction of your goal.

So how do you harness this power, overcome fear, and achieve these peak communicating experiences? It's a two-step process, and you begin by finding out where you are in the Four Stages of Speaking.

The Four Stages of Speaking

In my experience with thousands of business and professional people, I've found that there are four basic levels to communicating effectiveness. Each has different characteristics of *emotion, behavior, attitude,* and *position.* We all are in one of these four stages of speaking. What is important is to find out which one you are in, and to go beyond. We grow from Stage 1 to Stage 4 as we learn more about ourselves and our ability to control First-Brain fear, and as we practice, and as we speak.

STAGE 1: THE NONSPEAKER

- **Emotion.** Terror. These people are virtually scared to death of standing up and speaking before a group. Even the prospect of stating their name and introducing themselves before a group fills them with anxiety. Often nonspeakers are characterized by extreme shyness.
- **Behavior.** Rarely, rarely speak. Avoid speaking at all costs.
- **Attitude.** Passive, with excuses. "Gee, I'd love to, but I've got the flu." "Oops, that's my bowling night." "Sorry, got to take our goldfish to the vet." Occasionally Nonspeakers will get trapped into making a presentation at the office or giving a toast at a wedding, but

usually they are adept at making excuses to avoid presenting themselves publicly.

- **Position.** Support. Usually low skill level because they have little experience or ability as communicators, so they work in jobs that don't require communication skills.

Perhaps their job requires some speaking. Perhaps their spouse or a friend encourages them. For whatever reason, the Nonspeaker begins to blossom and graduates to the next stage. . . .

STAGE 2: THE OCCASIONAL SPEAKER

- **Emotion.** Fear. Not paralyzing fear, but sufficiently serious to limit their effectiveness. It is this fear that keeps them from volunteering. On those occasions when they are cajoled (or conned) into speaking, their nervousness usually shows.
- **Behavior.** Speak occasionally. They can be coaxed into taking a speaking assignment, but would never volunteer.
- **Attitude.** Active reluctance. Marked with growing awareness of the importance of communication. They probably know they must be able to present their ideas in order to get ahead—but they may not know how to go about it.
- **Position.** A frontline doer. Growing ability. Occasional Speakers are not locked into a pattern of hibernation and abject terror. They have tried public speaking—and they have survived. They have learned that they can improve with work.

With enough practice, the Occasional Speaker emerges as . . .

STAGE 3: THE WILLING SPEAKER

- **Emotion.** Tension. A trace of the old fight-or-flight response, but it's no longer a hindrance—more of an annoyance. Positive emotions pervade. Willing Speakers have learned to anticipate rather than dread the speaking experience. They find that extra edge of tension uncomfortable but stimulating, just like an athlete before a race. They know they will do well—but they're coiled and tensed for the performance, not complacent.

- **Behavior.** Speak often. They are vocal and articulate. They readily speak their mind in business meetings.
- **Attitude.** Willing. Butterflies—but they fly in formation.
- **Position.** Management. Proven ability. They may not think of themselves as "public speakers" but they have the skills to pull it off. And the confidence.

With enough motivation and experience they can become . . .

STAGE 4: THE COMMUNICATOR

- **Emotion.** Stimulation. Excitement about speaking. They are genuinely stimulated by speaking. They enjoy the feedback they get from the audience—not to mention the applause.
- **Behavior.** Speak always. First-Brain mastery. They have embraced the art of turning the fight-or-flight reaction into positive energy. Adrenaline is their ally.
- **Attitude.** Alacrity. Gusto. Enthusiasm. They don't hesitate to present themselves and their wonderful ideas. In fact, they jump at the chance! They know the rewards to be reaped.
- **Position.** Leadership. They are recognized for their ability to attract, persuade, and motivate people by the way they communicate. They inspire and command.

Whatever stage you are in, push on to the next stage. The way to do it is to just *do* it—using the power of the visualization principle.

The Visualization Principle

The way to conquer First Brain fear and put your New Brain in control of your First Brain is a technique called *visualization*. Visualization is not a new idea. It actually has its roots in the Bible. "As a man thinks in his heart, so he is," says Proverbs 27:19. Most of the success methods being sold today are based on some variation of this very real principle.

How does visualization enable us to master the First Brain? By transforming the emotive power of threatening situations into that of safe ones.

Maxwell Maltz, author of *Psycho-Cybernetics,* was an early exponent of the visualization principle. Almost half a century ago, he captured a truth that can literally transform the way we think, act, and communicate. He wrote,

> The mind cannot tell the difference between an actual experience and one vividly imagined.

Today we know that Maltz's statement can be refined even further: *The First Brain cannot tell the difference between an actual experience and one vividly imagined.* The New Brain can, but the First Brain cannot. *That* is the foundation of the visualization principle. *That* is why the visualization principle works.

The First Brain cannot distinguish reality from fantasy. That's why scary movies *really* scare us, even when our New Brain knows it's "only a movie." That's why bad dreams can awaken us with our hearts pounding and our sheets soaked with sweat. That's why just remembering an embarrassing childhood episode can make us blush, and just imagining jumping off the George Washington Bridge can make us short of breath and send a quiver of genuine terror up our spine. All of these experiences—a movie, a dream, a memory, an imaginary event—are forms of visualization (the movie is externally created, while the other experiences are generated in the New Brain).

Now you begin to see how powerful visualization is—and how it works to change the way the First Brain perceives and responds. We can create images in our minds that the First Brain will interpret as experiential reality. We can take a situation that the First Brain perceives as threatening and turn it into a cozy, warm, safe experience using nothing but the power of the imagination!

Some real-life examples will show you how it works in practice.

18 HOLES IN HIS BRAIN

Major James Nesmeth had a dream of improving his golf game and he developed a unique method of achieving his goal. Until he devised this method, he was just your average weekend golfer, shooting in the mid to low 90s. Then, for seven years, he completely quit the game. Never touched a club. Never set foot on a fairway.

Ironically, it was during this seven-year break from the game that Major Nesmeth came up with his amazingly effective technique for improving his game—a technique we can *all* learn from. In fact, the first time he set foot on a golf course after his hiatus from the game, he shot an astonishing 74! He had cut twenty strokes off his usual average without having swung a golf club in seven years! Unbelievable. Not only that, but his physical condition had actually deteriorated during those seven years.

What was Major Nesmeth's secret? *Visualization.*

You see, Major Nesmeth had spent those seven years as a prisoner of war in North Vietnam. During those seven years, he was imprisoned in a cage that was approximately four and a half feet tall and five feet long.

During almost the entire time he was imprisoned, he saw no one, talked to no one, and engaged in no physical activity. During the first few months he did virtually nothing but hope and pray for his release. Then he realized he had to find some way to occupy his mind or he would lose his sanity—and probably lose his life. That's when he learned to visualize.

In his mind, he selected his favorite golf course and started playing golf. Every day, he played a full eighteen holes at the imaginary country club of his dreams. He experienced everything to the last detail. He saw himself dressed in his golfing clothes. He smelled the fragrance of the trees and the freshly trimmed grass. He experienced different weather conditions—windy spring days, overcast winter days, sunny summer mornings. In his imagination, every detail of the tee box, the individual blades of grass, the trees, the singing birds, the scampering squirrels, the lay of the course became totally real.

He felt the grip of the club in his hands. He instructed himself as he practiced smoothing out his down-swing and the follow-through on his shot. Then he watched the ball arc down the exact center of the fairway, bounce a couple of times, and roll to the exact spot he had selected—all in his mind.

In the real world, he was in no hurry. He had no place to go. So in his mind he took every step on his way to the ball, just as if he were physically on the course. It took him just as long in objective time to play his game of mental golf as it would have taken in reality. Not a detail was omitted. Not once did he ever miss a shot, never a hook or a slice, never a missed putt.

Seven days a week. Four hours a day. Eighteen holes. Seven years. Twenty strokes off. Shot a 74.[1]

VIVIDLY IMAGINE

Maltz emphasized creating a successful self-image in your mind as a way to overcome low self-esteem. This will increase your confidence, and greater confidence naturally leads to increased energy and enthusiasm in communicating, and greater success in life. *Confidence is built on the experience of success.* The secret is to *vividly* imagine. And that experience can take place right in the corridors of our minds.

A vividly imagined visualization is not just a mental picture, not just a detailed mental picture, not just a mental picture with color and motion and sound. To be vivid, our mental image must be drenched with *emotion*. It is emotion that reaches the First Brain. It is emotion that saturates the memory storage centers of our brain so that the images we visualize become ingrained in us.

The key is to visualize those situations in which you have the greatest fear. As you visualize those situations, reframe them in your mind as *opportunities* to present yourself, to be successful, to change the direction of your life. You can use visualization in virtually any area of your life where you want to create change, improvement, and success.

Do you want to be a better parent? Begin by visualizing a trip to the mountains or the beach with your child. Or just playing catch in the backyard. Experience the *joy* of spending time with your child.

Have a problem with procrastination? Visualize getting that report handed in or that suitcase packed a day early. Experience the *satisfaction* of having an unpleasant task out of the way with time to spare.

Have a book in mind that you've always wanted to write but can't seem to get started? Then just take a page out of a book by my wife, Dru Scott.

VISIONS OF A BESTSELLER

Dru is a nationally recognized expert on customer satisfaction. She speaks, conducts workshops, and writes books on the subject. She is also an expert on the psychological success principles of time management, and wrote the bestseller *How to Put More Time in Your Life*.

During the year she spent actually writing the book, and long before she even had a publisher, she visualized herself in New York autographing copies near the curving staircase of a classy bookstore on Fifth Avenue. She imagined wearing a burgundy wool skirt and burgundy silk blouse with white pearls. In her mind, she experienced the excitement of having crowds hovering around her as she signed copy after copy of her bestselling book. She visualized the setting, the color, and the emotion of that book-signing party, and kept that image in front of her every day as she did the hard, lonely work of producing that book.

Her vision came true in every detail, including the pearls, the burgundy outfit—and the fact that the book was a phenomenal bestseller.

VISUALIZATION AND WORK

A golfer once said, "Visualize all you want, but if you don't know how to hit the ball, you can't beat a player who does." Visualization often gets a bad rap as if it were some sort of magic. It isn't, for it doesn't work without work—but it does work.

It gives us a psychological, emotional, and *conscious* goal and focus; it magnetically pulls us toward the achievement we desire.

For example, let's say I want to become a professional speaker. Anyone can lean back, put both feet up on the desk, and daydream about thunderous applause and rave reviews. But that's not visualization. Accolades and ovations don't go to the daydreamer but to the person with *drive*. And *discipline*. And *talent*. And *perseverance*. And even some *luck*.

So what's the difference between daydreaming and visualizing? Simple. Daydreaming is a substitute for work. But visualization *is* work. It's a *tool* you use to get the job done.

If I want to be a professional speaker, I can use the tool of visualization every time I get blocked or feel lazy or find myself procrastinating and not getting around to practicing or preparing a talk. I can visualize speaking to an audience of hundreds—and I can close with a visualized standing ovation. That gives me the focus and motivation to punch through the ennui, the laziness, and the pressures and make my "dreams" of a successful speaking career come true.

Visualization is no guarantee of success—but it gives you a visible target to shoot for. It powers your hard work. It motivates. It worked for Dru and for Major Nesmeth—but both brought considerable discipline, talent, and energy to the mix as well. Visualization is not just daydreaming. It's the battery that charges our engine so that we can do the *work* of making our dreams come true.

VISUALIZATION AND COMMUNICATION

Your vision of being a confident, powerful communicator can also come true. If you fear that next big speech or sales presentation, change the image in your mind. With your *consciously reasoning New Brain,* vividly imagine the setting. If it's a room or hall you've never been to before, try to visit it in advance so you can picture yourself speaking in that environment. If you can't see it beforehand, get a detailed description of the place. Bring as many senses into play as you can. Look at the surroundings, smell the carpet and the stale coffee, listen to the hum of the air conditioner, touch the lectern or the overhead projector.

Then comes the key part—vividly imagine how you will do and how you will feel. This is where the First Brain comes into play—the emotions. Put your feelings of success out there. You are going to be great! Imagine it. Rehearse it. And suddenly you *are* great! You feel it. You love the response. They are buying your concepts. They like you. You are triumphant.

You have only imagined it, but your First Brain gets it ingrained *emotionally*. The unreasoning part of your brain doesn't know the visualization is not real. It experiences your imagined triumph as *a real* event! That boosts your confidence—and increased confidence plus conscious preparation equals a *great* performance!

What if the reality turns out *not* to be everything you imagined? At the very least you can be sure it is a far sight better than it would have been if your mind had been filled with fear and negative thoughts. *And* you can be sure you have moved at least a step up the ladder of the Four Stages of Speaking.

Principles of Visualization

When you visualize:

1. **Make It Real.** Think of an upcoming communication event or recall a past successful event, and immerse yourself completely in that experience. Then add the five senses—touch, taste, sight, smell, and sound—and make the image real.
2. **Make It Positive.** Experience the sights and sounds of success. Bask in the applause. Practice imagining the experience perfectly. (Practice is only practice, but perfect practice makes perfect.)
3. **Make It Regular.** Do it daily. Find a regular time. A strategic time is at the start of the day—it sets up the day. Another is at bedtime, before you go to sleep—so your last thoughts can be positively working on your unconscious. If you are visualizing a successful talk before a large audience, envision that success before *every* speaking situation.
4. **Apply It to All Things.** One-shot visualization is like your first flying lesson—it may be fun, and get you up and back, but it won't take you very far. Make visualization your daily habit—applying to all things—then watch how your life changes. Successful people actually visualize before any major event. It is their habit to envision themselves achieving success and reaping the reward. Make it your habit too.

Just Do It

When all is said and done, the best way to get through the fear of speaking (or any other fear) is to face it head-on and *just do it*. But before you do it, visualize doing it perfectly, splendidly, to the acclaim of your listeners.

> *Do the thing you fear, and the death of fear is certain.*
>
> Ralph Waldo Emerson

Part V

From Information
to Influence

A t Decker Communications, we've always thought of our benchmark program as a Million-Dollar Seminar. Well that Million Dollar Seminar has actually now earned more than a hundred million dollars. More than a hundred thousand people have paid a thousand dollars each to attend our two-day communication training program, now called "Communicate to Influence."

It's not called "Communicate to Inform" for a reason. In today's world of information, people want to influence.

In the first edition of this book, and up to this point, I have emphasized the behavioral side of communications, because it is so critical in influencing others, and yet so seldom taught. In this revised edition I'm now going to add the message, or content, side of the communication equation. You really can't have one without the other, although it is useful to separate them to examine and learn the skills. So here, for the first time, you will have the complete book on speaking, as we marry our behavior with our content.

In the first nine chapters we dealt with the First Brain and its power. Although we never totally leave behavior and the First Brain and the influence of our unconscious over our communications perceptions and decisions, now we will take a look at our New Brain—our cerebral cortex—in more detail, and see how we can use it more effectively to create and maintain a focused, listener-based message.

Unfortunately, we are taught in our educational system that the spoken medium is an offshoot—a variation—of the written medium. That's just not so—they are totally different.

We are taught that if we say the words, people will get the message. Not necessarily.

We are taught that we should write out our speeches, and read them. Only if we want to put people to sleep.

If people aren't listening, they won't get our message—and too many listeners, particularly in business, are turned off or tuned out. And it doesn't have to be that way.

In Part V we'll learn how we can move from delivering information to influencing. We'll see how we can create a focused and listener-based message. You'll learn to think in terms of SHARPs to enliven *all* of your communications. And then we'll guide you on the final steps to mastering the entire communication process.

The final chapters on our journey in Part V are:

- **Chapter 10: The Power of Persuasion.** We are taught wrong, but we can learn how to influence people with the logic of our ideas and the emotional tone of our content. You'll see from a powerful new conceptual chart the principles that you can incorporate into your communications strategy.
- **Chapter 11: Creating Focused Messages.** The Decker Grid System that is an integral part of our training programs, which can help you stay on target with your messages, no matter what the subject. This simple but unique methodology becomes a way of thinking so that you can be more focused and effective in *all* of your communications.
- **Chapter 12: Creating Your Communications Experience.** You will learn to use the SHARP principles, so you will never again have to give a dull speech. More important, you will never have another dull communication interaction, as you will learn to continuously create a communication experience with your listeners, wherever you are.
- **Chapter 13: Mastery.** And in the final chapter, you'll take the final steps to mastery in all of your communications.

CHAPTER 10

The Power of Persuasion

On the first of January 2006 I named Steve Jobs the number one communicator of the year. (Each year the *San Francisco Examiner* publishes my list of the Top 10 Best [and Worst] Communicators of the Year, also at www.deckerblog.com). Jobs combines the best of both content and behavior—well prepared, focused, confident, and at ease.

In January of 2007 he did not disappoint again, as he gave a brilliant speech introducing the iPhone at Macworld. He was very influential. The day before, Bill Gates, chairman of Microsoft, gave a similar keynote on . . . uhm, actually, I forget what. He mentioned many things. He was very informative.

The press and the people lauded Jobs—and disregarded Gates. Here is what I said on my blog in reviewing the differences between the two:

> In their contrasting keynotes today and yesterday, there was **no contest** of course. Steve Jobs presents an experience and Bill Gates presents data. But it's worth a brief look to see their different approaches, so we can do the former, not the latter.
>
> Macworld has about 40,000 attendees in San Francisco, and the Las Vegas CES show has about 140,000 attendees. Yet Macworld gets equal or more press. Why? It's all due to Steve Jobs communicating an experience, and Bill Gates communicating

data. (It helps to have a new product like iPhone to talk about, but even in those years without breakthrough products, Macworld outdraws CES in publicity.)

- Here's one comment on Steve Jobs's keynote of today, from *Engadget*:

  "People are rapt, everyone is actually literally leaning forward and on the edge of their seat. We've never seen a presentation like this before."

  Jobs: "Isn't that incredible? Right on my PHONE! Look at this, the Eiffel Tower—isn't that incredible? Here's the last one, the Coliseum in Rome. Incredible new technology for entering text, a real browser on the phone, we can zoom in, Google maps, Widgets . . . it's the Internet in your pocket for the first time ever. You can't really think about the Internet without thinking about Google."

  And then he brings up Dr. Eric Schmidt, Google's CEO— great touch. (Also he brought up the CEOs of Yahoo and Cingular.)

- On the other hand, here's one comment on Bill Gates's CES keynote of yesterday, from the *Chicago Tribune* where Steve Johnson writes how "Bill Gates Serves Up an Infomercial."

  "Viewed charitably, Gates' 80 minute talk was a plea for a future in which all gadgets are interconnected, and Vista [Microsoft's new operating system] just happens to be at the center of that. But whenever there was a choice between emphasizing Vista and some more general notion of interconnectivity, the weight went to Vista. And 4,000 people left the room knowing little more than they had before, except, perhaps, that the biggest part of being magnificently rich lies in being willing to sell, sell, sell."[1]

Creating a Communication Experience wins every time.

That was my blog article. A few days later another article put it this way:

You would be forgiven for not knowing that Gates delivered a keynote address at the International Consumer Electronics Show (CES) in Las Vegas last week. Apple CEO Steve Jobs, speaking in San Francisco at the Macworld expo, stole all the attention from the Microsoft cofounder. Jobs had the Mac faithful—and technology journalists—eating out of his hand last Monday when he announced details of the long-awaited iPhone.[2]

You want to communicate to influence, not communicate to inform. As brilliant as Bill Gates is, he could have learned that lesson. But I'm not surprised, since few learn that lesson consciously.

We're Taught Wrong

We have one of the best educational systems in the world, but we are not taught to communicate. Oh, we're taught to read and write, but not to speak. We pick that up—and some of us get better at it by trial and error—by intuition and osmosis.

Reading speeches doesn't work (see Chapter 3), so we shouldn't write them out in the first place. Yet we are taught to write out speeches in our early years, and many people still read speeches.

I mentioned in Chapter 1 the disaster that struck politician Jeanine Pirro when she lost page ten of the speech she was reading. Most businesspeople don't read speeches, but most *do* go right to the Power-Points and in effect write out their content. Although it's slightly better in bullet and abbreviated text form, it is still in cognitive and linear mode. And how often do we see people using their PowerPoints as their notes? We want to say, "We don't need you speaking—we can read your notes as well as you can." (More on that in Chapter 12.)

We are taught that if we say the words, people will get them, but that is not necessarily true. They might get the words and our message if we are enthused and confident—but not if we're nervous and we block our message by inappropriate behavioral habits.

The written medium is a cognitive, linear, literal, and didactic process that is quite a bit different from the spoken medium. It's great for transferring information. You can read five times faster than you can hear, and five times faster than anyone can speak. It's efficient. You can reference data in the written medium, which is very useful for information, but not as powerful when you want to influence in person.

Speaking is the medium of action and influence. In speaking, we create an experience where people get *us and our message* together—and the two are inseparable. They will see and hear our enthusiasm, at the unconscious First-Brain level. In speaking, we use information to influence. The power is in the persuasion!

Look at the following chart. I call it the Create Your Experience chart, which shows the path that we can take from information to influence.

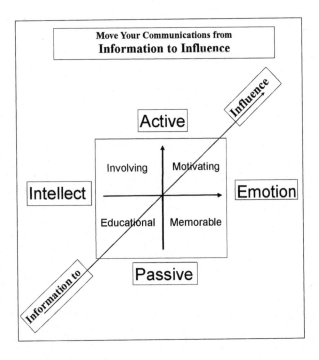

The Educational Process

Starting in kindergarten and continuing through college and into graduate school, we are taught passively. Basically we sit in chairs and teachers lecture at us. They appeal to our intellect, our cognitive side.

That is our educational system, and it continues into business and into life. It is the world of information. It is on the Passive and Intellectual sides of the chart.

Remember back in Chapter 7 when you thought of your favorite high school or college teacher? (If you don't remember doing that, take a moment now and think of the one teacher that most influenced you.) I'll bet you it wasn't necessarily the teacher with the longest tenure, the most research papers, or the most degrees after his or her name. I'll bet you it *was* the person who was the most excited about the subject, and that enthusiasm was contagious. You caught it, and because of that they influenced you to "get" the information and knowledge.

If we are effective, we use the process of the Educational quadrant, but we do more than that. We move people from passive to active, and from the intellectual to the emotional mental states.

The Involving Process

To move people from passive to active, we can do many things. One of the most important is to convey our energy and enthusiasm, which resonates in the listener. It's hard to be passive when someone is excited, but it's easy when someone is uninteresting, low on energy, and monotonous.

And there are several things we can do that deal more with content and process. We can ask questions, getting people to think. We can do interactive exercises, or take people through simulated exercises or thought processes. We can use fill-in-the-blanks in handouts. (Many say they do not like handouts—but they work. Tests have shown we remember far more when we write it down and we are involved.) We get people involved, and move them from passive to active, by interacting with them.

The Memorable Process

Moving people from the intellectual to the emotional realm is more difficult. We are not talking here about ignoring the intellectual or reasoning processes in the listener, but adding the emotional dimension to our content. We are not taught how to do this, but it is a very powerful mind-set that you can learn quickly and use continuously.

Emotional perspective comes from the energy of our behavior, of course, but it can also be applied in our content. We want to become memorable by using techniques and methods that get us out of the dry and didactic world of facts and figures. We want to use our creativity, to become storytellers and interesting visualizers, to move deeper into the world of ideation and metaphor.

We are talking about the SHARP principles, which are so important that we will devote all of Chapter 12 to them. SHARP is an acronym for the five key tools that are best understood and applied after creating our content, which we'll discuss in the next chapter.

The Motivating Result

The end result of this process is moving from information to influence. You will be able to more effectively persuade your listeners, not just by the power of your person, but by the power of your presentation as well.

In the next chapter, you can begin creating your message, giving it the life and vigor that comes from, and appeals to, the New Brain. This will then be a partner to the energy, confidence, and enthusiasm you have already learned to convey to your listener's First Brain.

CHAPTER 11

Creating Focused Messages

Adapting on a Moment's Notice

G uy Kawasaki, whom we met briefly in Chapter 6, is a marketing genius, hockey enthusiast, venture capitalist, blogger, and author. His books include *The Art of the Start* (2004), *Rules for Revolutionaries* (2000), *How to Drive Your Competition Crazy* (1995), and *The Macintosh Way* (1990). Guy was one of the Apple Computer marketing wizards who made the Macintosh so successful in the early 1980s. Today he is CEO of Garage Technology Ventures, which provides venture capital to high-tech start-up firms. Yet he still makes time, he says, "to pursue my bliss of writing, speaking, and consulting." He blogs three or four times a week (at www.blog.guykawasaki.com), writes a book every few years, and gives two or three speeches a week.

Over lunch, I asked Guy his secret of influencing and persuading people with the spoken word. "First, have something worthwhile to say. It's hard to be great at speaking if you don't have anything meaningful to say. Second, rehearse and repeat. I've given some of my speeches hundreds of times. It takes this many times to make it look spontaneous."

I asked Guy what his greatest asset as a speaker was. He replied, "I'm a quick study. I can adapt my speech to a specific audience very quickly. I often start prepping for a speech about thirty minutes before it starts. This short time frame makes it more challenging and exciting."

You may think, *Come on! Who does Kawasaki think he's kidding? How can anyone prep for a speech just thirty minutes before showtime?* I'm glad you asked—because I'm about to show you how you too, can give a compelling, persuasive talk on thirty minutes' notice—or even ten minutes' notice. I'll show you how you can start with nothing but a few ideas and some blank Post-it notes and create a focused, listener-based presentation that will move your audience to action.

The secret is the Decker Grid System.

Organized Yet Spontaneous: The Decker Grid System

The Decker Grid is a flexible invention that enables you to easily and consistently develop a message targeted on the needs and wants of the listener. It is specifically designed to call the listener to respond, to act, to get involved, or to buy. Think of it as software for the most powerful computer of all—your mind. Once you learn how to use the Grid, you will:

- Dramatically reduce the time it takes to produce a talk
- Increase the attention of your listeners
- Improve retention of the message by your listeners
- Speak confidently in every situation, even on a moment's notice
- Keep your presentations simple, brief, and focused on the essentials
- Dramatically increase your ability to persuade and motivate your listeners

When you use the Decker Grid System to create and deliver your presentations, you'll no longer speak merely to inform; you'll speak to persuade and motivate. You'll produce tangible results that enable you to reach the most important goals in your life. You'll no longer write out speeches, then read them to a bored audience while rooted in place behind a lectern. The Decker Grid frees you to deliver a brilliantly organized yet spontaneous conversation with your listeners.

How is all this possible? I'll show you. Let's look at the simple components of the Decker Grid.

TRIGGER WORDS

With the Decker Grid, you no longer write out a script. You don't write sentences at all. You use *trigger words*.

What does a trigger word trigger? Your mind! It jogs your memory. A trigger word may be one word, a short phrase, or even a simple picture or symbol. It stands for a fact, concept, story, or point that you could talk about for anywhere from half a minute to five minutes.

Let's say you want to give a talk about the health benefits of exercise. What kinds of trigger words might you use? Well, you know that exercise produces many benefits for the heart by lowering the risk of heart attacks, strengthening the heart muscle, reducing blood pressure, and maintaining the elasticity of the arteries. You know all of those facts, so you don't need to write them out. You just need a trigger word to remind you. And your trigger word doesn't need to be a literal word at all—a drawing of a heart will do.

And let's say you want to tell that funny story about the time you went flying off the treadmill while exercising. You can tell that story without a script. All you need is one trigger word, so you write *treadmill*.

The concept of trigger words is simple enough—but what do you write your trigger words on?

POST-IT NOTES

Trigger words go on Post-it notes—those little sticky paper notes. There are various brands of sticky notes, with the original Post-it notes made by the 3M company. The perfect size for trigger words is the 1½×2 inch size. Why Post-it notes? Because they allow you to:

- Stick them down anywhere
- Quickly move them around
- Add, edit, and create quickly

The flexibility of being able to move your ideas around in various configurations is what makes the Decker Grid so powerful.

How do you use your Post-it notes with the Decker Grid? Notice that they have a tendency to curl slightly—and if you stick them down the usual way, with the sticky end at the top, they curl away from you and are hard to read. So with the Decker Grid, you place your Post-it notes with the adhesive at the bottom. This way, the notes curl toward you and you can easily read the trigger words.

Next you'll need a tool to help you organize your ideas into an effective and persuasive presentation.

MESSAGE FOLDERS

The Message Folder is a preprinted tool available from Decker Communications (www.deckercommunications.com). The Message Folder helps you to:

- Brainstorm ideas for your talk
- Organize your ideas into a presentation that is both logical and persuasive
- Stay on point and on message as you speak

Steps to Using the Decker Grid System

There are four steps to preparing and delivering a message that makes an emotional connection with your listeners:

1. Lay the cornerstones
2. Create ideas (brainstorm)
3. Cluster the ideas into themes
4. Compose a message that motivates

The left- and right-hand pages of a Message Folder are shown on pages 214 and 215. The left-hand side of the Message Folder guides you in the first step—laying the cornerstones. The right-hand side serves as a guide to the composing step, the final edit of the message that connects with your audience and motivates them to buy into your message. Once your message is composed in that space, using your trigger words written on Post-it notes, you are ready to communicate your message to an audience.

The Decker Grid System is built upon a simple four-step process that we can think of as the four Cs of creating messages that motivate—cornerstones, create, cluster, and compose. Let's look at each of the four Cs in turn.

STEP 1: LAY THE CORNERSTONES

What are you going to talk about? Who is your audience? What do you want your audience to do? The cornerstones clarify and focus your thoughts so that you can persuade your audience to action.

Look at the Preparation Triangle on page 214. You'll see four rectangular cornerstone areas on the triangle—and just to the right of the triangle, you'll see a cloud. On a Post-it note, write the subject of your talk and place it on the cloud.

Why a cloud? Because clouds are nebulous and soft-edged. They have no hard corners. A cloud symbolizes the problem most of us have when we first start thinking about the talk we're going to give: We have a hazy idea of our subject, but we don't know precisely what we want to say about it. Our thinking is unfocused.

After we place the subject in the cloud, we lay the four cornerstones in the four rectangular spaces on the triangle. The cornerstones will clarify what we need to say and bring that cloudy subject into focus. The four cornerstones are:

- POV (point of view) how you feel about the subject
- Listeners: how they feel about you and your subject
- Action: what they should do about it
- Benefits: what's in it for them

Let's look at each of these four cornerstones, starting with:

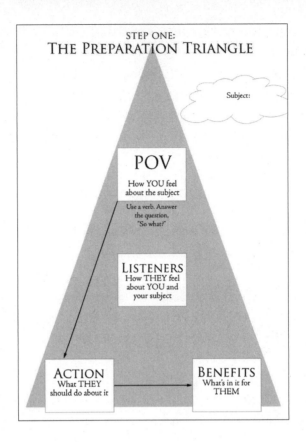

Cornerstone 1: POV. Your point of view is your attitude or opinion about the subject. Not sure what your POV is? Then ask yourself these questions:

- How do I really feel about this subject?
- What is there about this subject that makes me angry, excited, or passionate?
- What do I have at stake in this subject?
- What opinion or attitude do I want my audience to have about this subject?

A subject might be "Global Warming." A POV might be, "Global warming is destroying the planet." A subject might be "Golf." A POV might be "Everyone should play golf." A subject might be "Math Education." A POV might be "We need more math education."

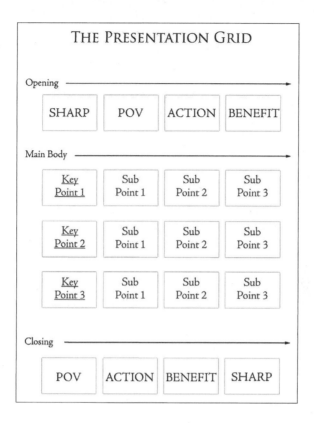

Assume that your audience starts with a "So what?" attitude. When you start speaking, your listeners will be asking themselves, "So what? Why should I care? What does this talk have to do with me?" Your POV should answer the "So what?" question. Not only will your POV put you in touch with your own feelings about the subject, but it will give your presentation a goal, an objective: The purpose of your message is to have your listeners leave the room sharing your emotions, your passions, your POV.

In as few words as possible (trigger words only!), write your POV on a Post-it note and place it in the POV space.

Cornerstone 2: Listeners. Who are your listeners? What is their perspective—their POV—on your subject? Are they likely to be open to your POV—or hostile? In your own mind, you can clarify who your audience is in terms of these categories:

- **D**emographics (the age, occupation, and cultural makeup of your audience)
- **N**eeds and interests of your audience
- **A**ttitudes of your audience toward you, your subject, and your POV

Demographics, Needs, and Attitudes—that's the DNA of your audience. Just as the physical makeup of a single human being is determined by biological DNA, the characteristics of your audience are determined by their DNA. Think very specifically about who your listeners are, their needs and interests, and their attitude toward your subject. Ask yourself: Will I have to overcome opposition, apathy, or resistance with my talk? Do I need to alter my approach in view of my listeners' age or occupation? How can I persuade them that the message I'm selling is exactly the message they need to buy?

Briefly describe your audience, writing your description on a Post-it note, and place it in the Listeners space.

Cornerstone 3: Action. Decide what you want your listeners to do after hearing your message. Do you want them to buy your book? Join your organization? Support your cause? It's not enough for people to be persuaded by your talk. You want them to demonstrate their agreement with your POV by springing into action and responding in a tangible way.

Actions should be clear and specific. An Action should be a concrete and measurable response to your talk, such as buying a product, ordering a subscription, signing a petition, or joining a club. The Action should be something that is done within a defined period of time—and the more immediate, the better. For example: "Right now, before you leave this room, I urge you to . . ."

Briefly describe that Action on a Post-it note and place it in the Action space.

Cornerstone 4: Benefits. People want to know "What's in it for me?" So tell them! Make sure your listeners know exactly how their lives will be improved when they buy into your message and respond by taking the Action you recommend. Benefits should be the natural consequences that accrue when people carry out the Action that you urge them to take.

Avoid generalities like "You'll be happier," or "The world will be a better place." Find specific benefits that will affect people's lives—their business lives, their family lives, their spiritual lives, their bank accounts, their safety and security. Remember your Listeners cornerstone, and find specific benefits that matter to them, based on their actual needs and interests.

Briefly describe the Benefits to your audience on a Post-it note and place it in the Benefits space.

STEP 2: CREATE (BRAINSTORM)

Many people consider this the most exciting, fun, and creative part of the process.

Place the Message Folder in front of you and focus your attention on the left side of the page, the Preparation Triangle. You've already placed your cornerstones, which establish the context of your message. You know your subject, your POV, your Listeners, the Action you want them to take, and the Benefits they will receive from taking those steps. Your mind is focused on what you want to accomplish.

The cornerstones give you the bare bones, the skeletal structure for your talk. Now let's hang some flesh on these bones. It's time to create a talk using the wealth of ideas, stories, and facts in your mind. It's time to create by brainstorming.

When you brainstorm, you sit down with a pad of Post-it notes and, for a defined period of time (say three to five minutes, no more than ten), you generate ideas—as many as you can, as quickly as you can. It is essential in brainstorming to set a time limit so you stimulate your mind to create rapidly—the time pressure is part of the process. You write down each idea as it comes, using only trigger words written on Post-it notes.

Focus on quantity, not quality. Generate as many ideas as you can. Don't criticize or edit your ideas, don't think in terms of good or bad. All you want is *lots* of ideas. Wild, crazy ideas are welcome. No idea is

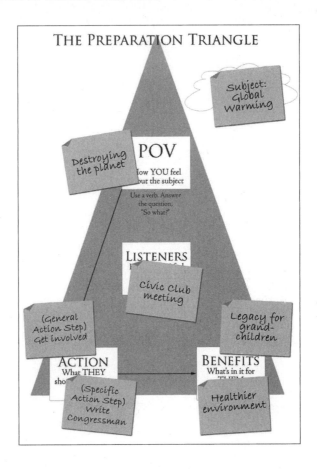

THE PREPARATION TRIANGLE

Subject: Global Warming

Destroying the planet

POV
How YOU feel about the subject

Use a verb. Answer the question, "So what?"

LISTENERS

Civic Club meeting

(General Action Step) Get involved

Legacy for grand-children

ACTION
What THEY should

(Specific Action Step) Write Congressman

BENEFITS
What's in it for THEM

Healthier environment

out of bounds. *Do not censor yourself!* You're engaged in a mental search and retrieval operation, and whatever pops into your consciousness is fair game: ideas, facts, statistics, stories, personal experiences, case histories, anything.

Scribble ideas as quickly as they come, rip them off the pad, plunk them down anywhere on the table. Neatness doesn't count. It's okay to make a disorganized mess. Creativity is messy and fun because it's completely uninhibited. Don't worry if your flow of ideas is chaotic. This is the time for chaos. You'll make order out of chaos later.

Keep brainstorming until your time is up. If the ideas are still flowing freely, take more time. Once you have assembled a mass of ideas, you're ready for the next step.

Sample of Step 1 (Cornerstones) and Step 2 (Create). See figures on page 214 and above for a sample of the first 2 steps in Preparation and Creating for the sample subject "Global Warming."

STEP 3: CLUSTER (IDEAS INTO THEMES)

Let's say you're preparing a talk on global warming. In your Create session, you brainstormed a chaotic mass of Post-it notes with such trigger words as CO_2, *extreme weather, Al Gore, carbon tax, S. Arrhenius, greenhouse gas, rising sea level, Roger Revelle, glacial retreat, mass transit, extinctions, Soylent Green, energy production, Siberian peat bogs, Clean Car Pledge, bike/walk, solar and wind, polar bear scare, ice-albedo feedback,* and so on (see figure above). Though all of those Post-it notes have *some* relationship to the subject of global warming, there's really no rhyme or reason to this jumbled collection of ideas.

Now it's time to bring order out of chaos.

As you look at this wilderness of ideas, you start to see connections. Many of these ideas have affinities for one another. Start clustering related ideas together in groups.

CO_2, *greenhouse gas,* and *energy production* are *causes* of global warming, so you pick up those Post-it notes and cluster them together. *Extreme weather, rising sea level, glacial retreat,* and *extinctions* are all *effects* of global warming; cluster them together. *Mass transit, Clean Car Pledge, bike/walk,* and *solar and wind* are *solutions* to the problem; cluster.

S. Arrhenius, Roger Revelle, and *Al Gore* are all people who have sounded an alarm about global warming; cluster them. There are some stories you can tell to keep your listeners involved—the *polar bear scare* story, the anecdote about the thawing *Siberian peat bogs,* and the analogy to the sci-fi movie *Soylent Green.*

After you're done clustering, you realize you have a few Post-it notes that don't fit with any others—for example, *ice-albedo feedback.* You look at your Listeners cornerstone and remember that your listeners will be a group of everyday folks at a civic club meeting—not a bunch of dummies, certainly, but not environmental scientists either. The *ice-albedo feedback* idea is too technical for this setting. Put that note aside.

If you have some leftover ideas that don't connect to other ideas, no problem. Don't force all the Post-it notes into clusters. Some simply won't fit. Ideas that don't cluster might be used later.

Once you've created a number of idea clusters, it's time to assign a label or title to each cluster. Write that label or title on a Post-it note, underline it for emphasis, and place it at the top of the cluster. These underlined labels will be your Key Points. The ideas clustered under these labels will be your Sub Points.

Review each cluster. These clusters will often trigger more ideas, so take a few minutes for additional brainstorming. After brainstorming, assign your new Post-it notes to the appropriate clusters.

Now you are ready to start the final editing or composing of your presentation.

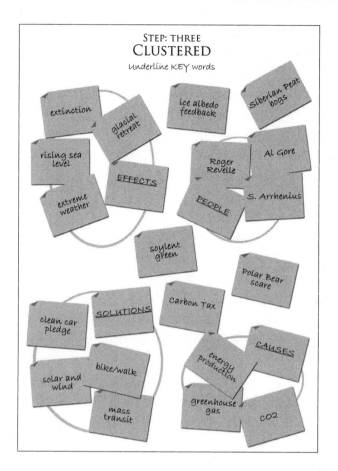

STEP: THREE
CLUSTERED
Underline KEY words

extinction

ice albedo feedback

Siberian Peat bogs

glacial retreat

rising sea level

Roger Revelle

Al Gore

EFFECTS

extreme weather

PEOPLE

S. Arrhenius

soylent green

Polar Bear scare

clean car pledge

SOLUTIONS

Carbon Tax

CAUSES

bike/walk

energy production

solar and wind

mass transit

greenhouse gas

CO2

STEP 4: COMPOSE A MESSAGE THAT MOTIVATES

The body of your message. In the Compose step, you pare down to your very best ideas and organize your presentation for persuasion and impact. Start by composing the central part of your message—the body. You'll compose the opening and closing later.

You'll use the KISS principle—Keep It Simple, Sweetheart (or Stupid, as the less genteel know this handy acronym). Stay away from data dumps by keeping to the essentials. You'll also use the Rule of Three—things are best remembered and organized in threes. Add a fourth item to any trio and retention plummets. As Muriel Humphrey once said to her husband, Vice President Hubert H. Humphrey, "Remember, Hubert, a speech doesn't have to be eternal to be immortal."

On the right-hand side of the Message Folder (see page 215), you'll see a layout for your presentation. That layout provides spaces for you to position your best three Key Points—and *only* three Key Points. To the side of each of those Key Points is a row of three spaces. Choose your three best Sub Points for each of those three Key Points.

People won't be able to absorb every detail, only the main points, so keep it simple. The layout of the Message Folder is designed to follow the Rule of Three.

Old Communicators engage in the dreaded data dump, swamping their listeners with facts and information. But you, as a New Communicator, want to make an emotional connection. You seek to persuade your listeners to your POV and move them to action. Dumping a truckload of information on them only undermines your likability and turns your listeners against your point of view. So resist the temptation to deliver four or more points. Stick with three and be memorable.

Prioritize your Key Points. Often, your first Key Point is introductory. You lay out the problem to be solved or the background of the issue you're discussing. Structure your talk so that you build to your strongest and most important Key Point. You want to make a big impact at the beginning—but you want to save your maximum impact for the end.

As you Compose, you'll find that the Decker Grid gives you enormous freedom and flexibility. You can trade Sub Points in and out, move ideas around, and rearrange your Key Points in seconds—just by moving your Post-it notes.

The beginning of your message. Once you have the main body of your message, it's time to go back to the beginning and compose the opening of your talk. A good opening is critical to setting the tone for your message and giving your listeners a reason to listen.

There are many ways to begin your message, and the Decker Grid enables you to create an opening with impact—an opening that will prepare your listeners to be persuaded. The basic opening outlined in the Decker Grid consists of your POV, a general Action step, and a brief Benefits statement. In other words, you give your listeners a road map at the beginning of your talk, telling them where you are taking them, how you will want them to respond (stated in a broad, general way), and the Benefits that will be theirs as a result. By communicating the Benefits up front, you give the listeners an incentive to listen.

In Chapter 12, we will focus on attention getters called SHARPs that you can use at the very beginning (and at other points in your talk) to grab and hold the attention of your listeners. Looking at the Compose page of your Message Folder, you'll see a space at the beginning of your talk labeled SHARP. For now, we will leave the SHARP space blank, but we will come back to it later.

The closing of your message. The closing structure outlined in the Message Folder is easy to create and effective when delivered. In

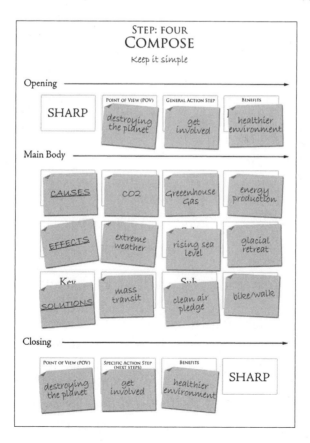

Chapter 12, we'll add a SHARP to the ending to serve as a "memory hook," a big emotion-triggering finish to make the ending of your speech memorable and powerful. For now, we'll leave the final SHARP space blank.

In the basic closing, you sum up the features of your message: You restate your POV. You tell your listeners the Action step(s) you want them to take (this time, you state the Action specifically, not broadly and generally as you did in the opening). Finally, you restate the Benefits your listeners will receive by taking those Action steps.

Look at page 223 and you will see a completed sample "compose" page for the subject of global warming.

Again, remember the Rule of Three. Ideally, it's best if you can state *three* specific Benefits that your listeners will receive by taking the Action steps—and state them as tangibly and enthusiastically as possible: "There are so many benefits to our service, but in closing, let me list three: One, you'll have absolutely limitless income potential. Two, you'll have fourteen more hours a week to spend with your family. Three, you'll be saving the planet—and won't *that* make you feel warm and fuzzy inside!"

Remember, your last statement to your audience is the most memorable. Make sure it's a powerful statement that motivates your listeners to *Action*.

Final check. After you have composed your message—body, opening, and closing—go back and review your cornerstones. Ask yourself: Have I constructed a message that meets the needs of my Listeners? Have I taken into account the DNA of my audience (Demographics, Needs, and Attitudes)? Have I stated my POV clearly, so that my listeners can buy into my POV? Have I stated the Action in such a way that my listeners know *exactly* what to do in response to my message? And are the Benefits clear so that my listeners will be enthusiastic and motivated?

That's it! You've composed a winning presentation that will be engaging, memorable, and persuasive—and it has taken minutes instead of hours to do so. When you deliver this presentation, you'll be natural and spontaneous, because you won't be reading from a script—you'll be having a natural conversation with your listeners. You'll never get lost, because you won't be reading, you'll be communicating. If you happen to hit a snag and you forget what comes next, a quick glance at your trigger words gets you instantly back on track—and your audience will never notice that anything was wrong. Imagine the confidence you'll feel giving presentations from the Decker Grid!

Now there's just one more piece of the Grid to put in place, and you'll be ready to shine. You just need to add a few attention getters and memory hooks to your presentation. We call these simple yet powerful attention getters "SHARPs"—and that's what we're going to learn in the next chapter.

Creating Your Communication Experience

Attention Getters and Memory Hooks

Ronald Reagan intuitively understood that giving a great speech requires more than merely saying words and dispensing information. He knew that communicating is about making an emotional connection—and he used many attention getters and memory hooks to make his point.

On February 5, 1981, in his first televised speech after becoming president, Mr. Reagan talked about how inflation had devastated the American economy. He held up a dollar bill in one hand. "Here is a dollar such as you earned, spent, or saved in 1960," he said. Then he held up a few coins in the other hand. "And here is a quarter, a dime, and a penny," he said, "thirty-six cents. That's what this 1960 dollar is worth today."

Watching the speech, one of the president's Democratic Party rivals remarked, "It takes an actor to do that! Jimmy Carter would have emphasized all the wrong words. Jerry Ford would have fallen under the desk. And Dick Nixon would have pocketed the cash!"

Reagan knew what many speakers have still not figured out: If you want to keep your listeners' attention and make a lasting impression, use attention getters and memory hooks. Research shows that people remember the first and last points of a presentation more clearly and vividly than anything that is said in between. So make sure you snag your listeners' attention at the beginning, perk your listeners' First Brains up several times in the middle, and wow them at the end.

When you stand before an audience, remember their needs and wants. Your presentation may be the third or fourth talk they've had to sit through. They may be bored or reading the newspaper or instant messaging their significant others. They may be caffeine-deprived— and they are probably suffering from information overload.

And consider this: The average adult attention span is only eight seconds. *Eight seconds!* That means that you can lose them in eight seconds. If you are not interesting and memorable, people will tune out.

SHARPs: Bringing Emotion into Content

Don't make your listeners work hard to stay awake, involved, and interested. You can *rivet* the attention of your listeners' First Brains if you know the simple secret of the SHARP principles. SHARP stands for:

> S —Stories and examples
> H—Humor
> A—Analogies
> R —References and quotations
> P —Pictures and visual aids

You may not need all five SHARPs. In fact, most people find that two or three of the SHARP principles work best and fit naturally with their style of communicating. Let's look at each of the SHARP principles and you can decide which ones work best for you.

S—STORIES AND EXAMPLES

Storytelling is one of the oldest and most reliable aids a speaker has for holding the interest of an audience and illustrating important points. Before the printed word, people passed on wisdom and custom through storytelling. In that greatest best seller of all time, the Bible, we have two vivid examples.

Jesus told stories and parables. He didn't talk in concepts—he only needed stories, and he riveted people's attention: sowing seeds along the path, the rich young ruler, a house built on sand, faith growing like a mustard seed, and dozens more.

Another model is the apostle Paul, who often used this SHARP to open his speeches. In Acts 17, Paul walks through the Greek city of Athens and he sees that the city is filled with idols. So Paul goes up to Mars Hill, the place where all the Greek philosophers gathered to debate the great philosophical issues of the day.

"Men of Athens!" Paul says. "I see that you are all very religious. As I walked around and examined your objects of worship, I even found an altar with an inscription that reads, 'To an Unknown God.' Now, I'm going to proclaim to you the God you know only as something unknown." And Paul proceeds to tell the Athenian philosophers about his God.

It was a tough crowd, and the book of Acts records that some of the Greeks sneered at his message—but many others said, "We want to hear you speak on this subject again!" Some were even persuaded—by Paul's POV, the Action he recommended, and the Benefits he promised—to become followers of Paul's God. It all began with a SHARP, a story, an example of an altar that Paul had seen while walking through the city.

We all have personal experiences and examples we can draw upon to add emotion and excitement to our messages. Real-life experiences are the most memorable because they have the deepest emotional impact. But hypothetical examples, allegories, and even fairy tales can be effective ways to make a memorable point as well.

Pat Williams, the vice president of the Orlando Magic we met earlier, says, "Stories create mental pictures and illustrate principles in a way that makes your message unforgettable. When I speak before groups, I always keep an eye on the nonverbal feedback from the audience. If I see anyone beginning to yawn or check his watch, I use a simple line that always perks them up: 'Now, let me tell you a story. . . .' Works every time."

Make sure that the story you tell has an obvious connection to your subject, however. In fact, after you tell the story, it helps to underscore the connection so that the listener doesn't have to wonder *What does that have to do with . . . ?*

Now, during the Create phase, as you were brainstorming ideas for your presentation, you probably thought of a number of great stories for your talk. But if not, then after you have composed your talk, take time to think of some stories and examples that will apply to your message and support your points. Remember to indicate your stories on Post-it notes using only trigger words.

For example, let's say I'm giving a talk on SHARPs, and I decide to open my speech with this story about a former president's use of humor: "While campaigning for reelection in 1944, President Franklin Delano Roosevelt was accused of wasting taxpayer money by sending a naval destroyer all the way to Alaska just to pick up his Scottie dog. Roosevelt responded to the charge by saying, 'I don't mind hearing the Republicans lie about me, but I bitterly resent their libelous statements about my dog!' "

Now, what trigger word would I write on my Post-it note as a reminder of that story? I would simply write "FDR."

You don't need to have your stories and examples written out. Just tell your stories as you would if you were chatting with someone over coffee. Don't worry that you'll flub up the story. You're a natural storyteller—all people are! When you're in front of your audience, that single trigger word is all you'll need to prompt your recall. Then just tell the story the same way you'd tell it by the water cooler or over coffee with a friend. If you tell the story naturally and conversationally, you'll tell it with impact.

H—HUMOR

In July 2002, Canadian comic actor Mike Myers, of Austin Powers fame, was honored with a star on the Hollywood Walk of Fame. After receiving the plaque and having his picture taken next to the star, it was Myers's turn to give a short acceptance speech. Glancing at the X-rated gift shop behind him, Myers began, "It's a long way from playing street hockey in Toronto to having a star in front of the International Love Boutique."

Whether or not you have a star on Hollywood Boulevard, it's a good idea to use humor in your talks. You say you're not good at telling jokes? Perfect! Hardly anybody is! So don't tell jokes. Instead, add a light touch of natural humor to your message. Humor is humanization. Gentle, tasteful humor, adroitly used, adds energy to your talk and makes you more relaxed, comfortable, and likable. It's a powerful tool in helping you to connect with your audience.

It's virtually impossible to dislike someone who makes us laugh. A sense of humor—whether sharp, explosive, dry, or witty—makes you appear more genial, warm, and memorable. Our First Brains use strong emotions—including the emotions that accompany laughter and smiles—to saturate our New Brains with vivid impressions that increase retention of the message.

Here's a classic example—under pressure: In 1984, seventy-six-year-old Ronald Reagan was running for reelection against fifty-six-year-old Walter Mondale. Reagan knew that his age was a concern in the campaign. A fumbling performance against Mondale in the first debate had created the impression that Reagan was a bit foggy. So Reagan was ready when a reporter served up the age question in the second debate.

"I will not make age an issue of this campaign," Reagan replied. "I am not going to exploit for political purposes my opponent's youth and inexperience."

The press and the audience howled. Even Mondale couldn't repress a laugh—even though Reagan's quip had effectively doomed Mondale's election hopes. The age issue never came up again, and Reagan's humorous reply was considered the most memorable event not only of that debate—but of all the presidential debates.

What's your sense of humor like? A dry, subtle wit? The ability to poke gentle fun at yourself? A flair for earthy, gut-level humor? A unique outlook on everyday life? Do you find unexpected amusement in the things that happen around your home or office? What kinds of things do you do and say in private conversations that make people laugh? How can you work them into your presentations?

Humor is the hardest communication skill to exercise—but one of the most effective. Think funny. Keep a journal of wry observations,

Think funny

funny quotations, and stories. Look for the humor in the serious—it's almost always there.

People like to laugh—and they love those who make them laugh. The key to using humor is to let the lightness flow naturally—don't force it. Go for positive energy, not belly laughs.

A—ANALOGIES

The human mind continually compares, contrasts, categorizes, and cross-references. This natural human function creates analogies— verbal comparisons of the similar features of two dissimilar things. Analogies are useful in making unfamiliar concepts understandable by comparing them to things people already understand.

In the film *Working Girl,* Tess McGill (Melanie Griffith) is a secretary working in lower Manhattan. A streetwise plain talker from Staten Island, Tess feels intimidated by the glib, sophisticated Wall Street types all around her. During a complex negotiation for a big corporate merger, Tess's straight talk causes an uproar. The deal collapses. Tess is in hot water. At that point, the head of the company comes to Tess's rescue with this analogy:

"There was a story on the news last night," he says. "Seems a truck got stuck at the entrance to the Holland Tunnel. Too high for the clearance. Well, for hours the experts tried to find some way to un-wedge the vehicle, but to no avail. Finally, a ten-year-old girl in a passing car suggested simply letting the air out of the tires to lower the truck to clearance level, which they did. And it worked. Well, by letting some of the air out of our merger plans, Miss McGill has effectively shown all of us the light at the end of our tunnel."

That analogy was a key turning point in the movie.

Analogies are often used to simplify technical concepts. For example, analogies are commonly drawn between brains and computers, even though a human brain is dissimilar to a computer in most respects. A brain is an organ of the body, made up mostly of water, serving as the control system for the central nervous system. A computer is a machine made of metal, silicon, glass, and plastic, used to manipulate data according to programmed instructions. Yet because both a brain and a computer process information, a brain is often said to be "like a computer" and a computer is often said to be "like a brain."

The heart is often the subject of analogies. Prosaically, the human heart is like a water pump—but poetically, it is also like a bottle containing emotions or a chapel where God dwells.

Some analogies—especially historical analogies—can be sobering (and controversial), as when Senator Edward Kennedy said in a 2004 speech at the Brookings Institution, "Iraq is George Bush's Vietnam." To compare *anything* to Vietnam is to summon a haunting image of America's most costly and tragic foreign policy failure.

But analogies can also be very funny, as when comedian Dennis Miller observed, "Congress is to lying what Wisconsin is to cheese."

Analogies not only perk up listener interest, but they can make complex ideas simple, understandable, and memorable. To develop an analogy, ask yourself how your subject or concept is like something else. The similarities could be physical, metaphorical, or functional.

Write your analogies in brief trigger words on Post-it notes and save them with your other SHARPs. Vary the types of analogies you use. Don't draw all your analogies from a single field, such as sports or history.

Be sensitive to your listeners cornerstone. Think about the "DNA" of your audience, and remember that some analogies may not be well received by people of certain age groups or political persuasions or cultural backgrounds. Choose analogies that are positive and that will make an emotional connection with your listeners.

R—REFERENCES AND QUOTES

You've got to be believed to be heard—and one way we insure that we are believable is by fortifying the content of our message with references and quotations. A reference is any independent source of information that you cite in order to support your Key Points and Sub Points. It can be facts, data, statistics, or other supportive information from publications (magazine articles, trade journals, newspapers), broadcast sources (radio or TV), or responsible Internet sites. (Keep in mind that there is a lot of material on the Internet that is irresponsible, unreliable, and just plain wacky.)

And what about quotations? Writer George Alec Effinger once wrote, "Ambrose Bierce defined a 'quotation' as, 'The erroneous recitation of another person's words.' Or words to that effect."

Quotations are selected statements that lend support and credence to your argument. Usually, quotations come from famous people or noted experts in a given field, but they may also come from such sources as advertising campaigns, song lyrics, movie dialogue, and other pop culture sources. The best quotations for a spoken presentation are pithy, concise, and easy to understand. Audiences easily get lost in quotations that are too long or stated in a convoluted way. Your local bookstore carries books of quotations on various subjects, and these resources can be handy aids to assembling a presentation that motivates.

The only time you should ever read during a spoken presentation is when you are citing references and quotations. Go ahead, put your glasses on your nose, and read it verbatim. Make sure you don't misquote anyone or get your facts wrong. You want the audience to know that you are being careful with all of your references.

P—PICTURES AND VISUAL AIDS

As we noted in Chapter 6, the Eye Factor—the visual sense— dominates *all* the senses. To communicate effectively, you must speak the language of the First Brain, which is a visual language. A spoken message that is visually reinforced has greater impact and believability than a spoken message alone.

Pictures, objects, charts in PowerPoint presentations, and other visual aids are powerful SHARPs that enable you to communicate with impact and persuasion. You can use visual aids to organize complex data into simple, understandable graphs and tables that will complement your personal energy and the verbal content of your message. Research shows that:

- Retention increases from 14 to 38 percent when listeners see, as well as hear, a presentation.
- Presentations using visual aids are 43 percent more persuasive than unaided presentations.
- Group consensus is 21 percent higher in meetings in which visual aids are incorporated.
- The time required to communicate a concept can be reduced up to 40 percent with the use of effective visuals.

PowerPoints have become ubiquitous, and are a great tool to design and deliver visuals that beautifully complement your spoken presentation, if done right. The benefits of computer-based visuals include: a wide range of color and graphic formats, the flexibility to make last-minute changes, and the ability to combine charts, graphs, images, music, and video clips with your talk.

Beware of PowerPoint abuse, however, which is an epidemic in business. Too many people make their PowerPoints their presentations, using them as their notes, with too much text, too many bullets, and just too much. And some people get so gadget-happy that they try to wow the audience with dazzling special effects, resulting in visuals

USE BLACK SLIDES

PowerPoints are great—used correctly. The problem is that 95 percent of the time we run into PowerPoint abuse.

If you follow just *one* rule, it can transform the way you present information to influence using PowerPoints (or PPs, as they are getting pretty generic).

Use Black Slides

There are three reasons, but first the context.

The problem with PPs is that they become the presentation itself, and that lends itself to delivering information, and data dumps. In most business settings it's almost like reading a manuscript as someone puts up PP after PP and uses them as notes. (Rule of Thumb with PPs—less is more!)

A black slide is literally a slide with no master and a black background. (It is not the "B" key, which will blank out a slide, but you always have to unblank and go back and show the old slide before you can continue on.)

A black slide will do three things:
1. **Clear the screen.** Once you're done with the picture, graph, or supporting information, you want to remove the distraction and go to a black slide so you can amplify, tell a story, or make an additional point.

that drown out the message. Other people are just not very good at PowerPoints, so they produce visuals that are poorly designed and distracting.

Low-tech tools, such as flip charts, are still effective for getting your point across in a visual way. Some of the best visual aids I've seen have been the simplest of props—a ball of yarn and scissors or a bowl of fruit. I've also seen people use special talents to add visual flair to a speech—everything from juggling to singing to sleight of hand.

When developing your visual aids, remember the Three *B*s: Make them Big (so everyone can see them), make them Bold (bright color, a lot of contrast), and keep them Basic (less is more.)

(continued)

2. **Black out the screen.** This lets you walk in front of the projector. Almost all meeting, board, and conference rooms are poorly designed so that they have the projector screen right in the middle of the room or stage. It should be at the right or left, so *you* can be in the middle. After all, *you* should be the center of your presentation, not your slides.
3. **Totally change your mind-set.** Change the creation and emphasis of the presentation. This is by far the most important of all, and needs its own paragraph.

Philosophy of the Black Slide

I'd estimate that 95 percent of business presentations are poorly conceived in that they are created in PowerPoints. This may be easier, but it is not more effective. If you realize that your information and your PPs are *not* your presentation, but *you* and your Key Points are, then you will create your presentation first and use PPs to amplify your Point of View (see Chapter 11.) Then PPs will be used effectively, with graphs, pictures, video clips, and other SHARPs to bring memorability and power to your Point of View.

When you *think* black slides, you will put together your PPs after you create and organize your thoughts—and using the Decker Grid is the ideal way to do that. Then your PowerPoints will be additive (and not essential). Only when you think in terms of black slides will you be freed up from PowerPoint abuse.

When you use black slides, you will bring light to your listeners, and most likely win them over to your Point of View.

Putting It All Together

Ideas for SHARPs may occur to you at any stage of the preparation process. Actually, you should think of SHARPs as a way of communicating—intersperse SHARPs in all your communications. When you are in the Create (brainstorming) stage of using the Decker Grid, you'll think of stories, funny lines, and analogies that fit your content and POV. Jot them down as trigger words during your brainstorming session; then Cluster them in one place under the heading "SHARPs." As you are Composing your talk, more SHARPs will occur to you: "This would be a good place for that Mark Twain quotation," or, "I'll need to illustrate this concept with some PowerPoint graphs."

When those ideas come to you, jot them down as trigger words and Cluster them under "SHARPs."

Later, after you have your talk composed on the Decker Grid layout, you'll have an overview of your entire talk—beginning, middle, and end. You can see at a glance all the best places to position your SHARPs. You'll see the flow of your message, and you'll have a clear sense of which SHARP would open your talk with a bang, which would close it on a resounding high note, and which ones would be great at intervals to give your talk a rhythm and keep your listeners involved. At that point, you can pick up your SHARPs Post-it notes and place them on the Decker Grid—and you'll have your speech composed and ready to deliver.

Take advantage of the amazing flexibility of the Decker Grid. If you find that one of your Sub Points doesn't work or you need to move some ideas around, you can! It's easy. You can edit your talk even as you rehearse it. After a couple of practice runs, try giving your talk before a camcorder. Time it and see if you need to make adjustments to your content or delivery. Fine-tune your message. Build your confidence. In time, you'll find that the Decker Grid is endlessly adaptable to different situations.

One day, someone may take you aside at a big meeting and whisper in your ear, "Smith was supposed to do the keynote address, but he's down with the flu! Could you get up and talk for ten minutes about our company's values? You're on in twenty minutes!"

You weren't expecting to speak, so you don't have the Decker Grid with you—your Message Folder is at home on your desk. No problem! The Grid is so simple, you already have it where it counts—right between your ears. So you grab an envelope or a cocktail napkin and you quickly lay the four Cornerstones—your POV, Listeners, Action, and Benefits. You brainstorm some ideas for your talk, then you quickly Compose those ideas on a hastily drawn Grid, plug in a few SHARPs here and there, run through it one time in your mind, and—

You're on!

And for ten minutes, you're brilliant, magnificent, and persuasive!

At the end, the applause is thunderous, because you have made an emotional connection with every First Brain in that room.

That's the power of the Decker Grid System and the power of SHARPs. With the power of the Grid in your hands and in your mind, you're ready to take on the world. Now, mastery.

CHAPTER 13

Mastery

The Master of Confident Living

It was a blustery spring day in New York City when I first met Dr. Norman Vincent Peale. Dr. Peale was, of course, the author of nearly fifty books, including *The Power of Positive Thinking,* which has sold twenty million copies in more than forty languages. I visited him in his charming office across from the Museum of Modern Art off Fifth Avenue. At age ninety-two he was vigorous and hearty, and his handshake was firm. He told me he was leaving the next day to give a speech in Toronto.

We sat and talked, and he told me the surprising story of how he went from being painfully shy and insecure to becoming the world's foremost proponent of confident living. "I was an anomaly," Dr. Peale told me. "I had no confidence at all, and I was shy to extreme pain. I was what they call bashful.

"Oh, I'll never forget Ben Arneson. After he talked to me I went down the stairs from the classroom and I stopped on the fourth step from the bottom—it's still there on that campus—and I set up my kind of a prayer meeting. I said, 'Dear Lord, you can take a drunk and make him sober. You can take a thief and make him honest. Can't you also take a mixed-up young fellow like I am and make me normal? I believe you will do it. Thank you very much. Amen.'

"Then I expected a miracle to happen—and a miracle did happen over time. At that moment I felt strangely peaceful and sort of happy. I believed that He was going to do this for me and change me. Then the next day a professor of English, my major, called me into the office and said, 'Peale, what do you know about Emerson?' I said, 'Not much, Professor.' 'Well,' he said, 'I am giving you this book to read and I want you to observe that what Emerson teaches is the sovereignty of the human mind when it is working.'

"Then later I discovered on my own a book by William James, who was the father of American psychology. He said that the greatest discovery of this generation is that the human being can alter his life by altering his attitudes of mind.

"I took myself by the nape of the neck and I said, 'Get with it.'

"I've stood outside the wings of many a hall when I was being introduced and I talked myself into going out there with extreme confidence and talking about confidence and I made myself confident by *talking* about it—and then *acting*."

With his newfound confidence, Norman Vincent Peale became a minister, a sought-after public speaker, and a world leader, bringing hope and a positive view of life to millions of people.

Confident to Communicate

As Dr. Peale's life shows, confidence is the key to effective communicating—and to living an effective, successful life. We have trained hundreds of thousands of people in the Decker Method. Most of them have an abundance of ability but a shortage of confidence. In fact, I would have to say that I have not met one person who entered the program with an accurate picture of how he or she came across to others. Saddest of all, virtually all of these people thought they were *less* than they truly are. Less attractive. Less capable. Less competent. Less talented. Less articulate.

Like the young Norman Vincent Peale, they were insecure and even downright shy—yet I could see that they had the potential to achieve far more than they imagined. I have found over the years that my primary challenge as a coach is not to impart communicating skills or to teach techniques. My biggest challenge is to help people to see themselves more accurately and build their confidence.

This was the same challenge faced by Dr. Maxwell Maltz, a cosmetic surgeon and author of several books, including his longtime bestseller *Psycho-Cybernetics*. One of Dr. Maltz's early patients was an eighteen-year-old girl named Helen. She came to him with a severe scar on her left cheek, the result of an auto accident.

Dr. Maltz operated on her, and when he removed the bandages he was delighted to see that her skin was flawless. "Helen," he said to her, "look at yourself in the mirror. What do you see?"

The girl looked for a long time without a word. Then she whispered, "Doctor, I don't see any difference."

Maltz was shocked. He then showed the girl a photo of herself taken before the surgery, clearly showing the ugly scar. Holding the photo and the mirror side by side, he said, "Now do you see the difference?"

Again the girl was silent for a long time. Finally, she said, "Doctor, I see that the scar is gone, but I don't feel *any* different."

That was a moment of revelation for Maxwell Maltz. He had stumbled on a profound truth: Fixing people on the outside doesn't fix them on the inside. The insecurity and poor self-image that many people have goes far deeper than a deformity of the flesh. That discovery launched Maltz into a new profession: helping people change the way they see themselves. It became his lifelong mission.

And that's my mission, too. I want people to see themselves more accurately so that they will have the confidence to communicate and achieve their dreams and goals. I want people to know that they are better, more competent, and more articulate than they think they are. The power to see ourselves accurately and objectively is one of the most transforming truths of human existence.

The key to seeing ourselves as other people see us is a principle I call "video-cybernetics."

Video-Cybernetics

Maxwell Maltz took the title of his book *Psycho-Cybernetics* from the word *cybernetics,* coined in 1948 by the mathematician Norbert Wiener from the Greek word *kybernetes,* meaning "steersman." Cybernetics is the science of control functions in human beings and mechanical systems. The basic principle of cybernetics is this: When a human being or a mechanism is not functioning correctly, it's because the human or mechanical control system is receiving negative or false feedback. In order to correct the problem, negative feedback must be replaced by positive feedback.

Psycho-cybernetics seeks to replace negative psychological feedback with positive thinking. Video-cybernetics takes the science of cybernetics a step further. Instead of replacing negative feedback with subjective positive thinking, video-cybernetics replaces negative feedback with objective sound and images. People who are stuck in negative thinking and behavior patterns are able to see themselves objectively on video and discover that they are much better communicators than they think they are. Positive video feedback is a powerful corrective to the negative psychological feedback that hinders and inhibits us.

Roger was a sales engineer with a national transportation company who went through the Decker training program. Video-cybernetics transformed Roger's image of himself. "Seeing myself on video was an eye-opener," he said. "I've always been hard on myself after speaking before a group. I'd think, 'Well, I sure blew that one.' But after seeing the video playback, I realized I looked pretty good. That was the biggest confidence builder of the whole seminar."

Gwen, the director of children's ministries in a large California church, recalled, "I was really nervous the first day of the seminar. During my first talk, I felt shaky inside. But I watched the videotape later and I couldn't see a hint of nervousness! I took the tape home and showed it to my kids and they said, 'Mom, you look confident! Weren't you nervous?' Seeing myself on video really did a lot for my self-assurance."

My wife, Dru Scott Decker, is a professional speaker and she testifies to the power of video feedback. "I used to fly to the East Coast, give a presentation, then spend the entire flight back to the West Coast thinking of all the things I could have done better. I'd make a list of twenty or so things that needed to be improved.

"What's been fascinating is to see my presentations on videotape. Sure, I still find twenty things that could have gone better. But I also see two hundred things I did well! That's what's useful—having that balanced and positive perspective that video gives.

"I had a session taped that I did in the Bay Area. The group was relatively quiet. During the talk I felt rusty and not too effective. I thought I had turned in a poor performance until I saw the tape. Then I thought, 'That's sensational! I did a great job!' I needed to see the two hundred things I did well in order to put the twenty rough edges into perspective. And the next week the meeting executive said, 'Absolutely on target,' confirming my own impression. So I am a real believer in video feedback."

Camcorders are now ubiquitous. Most people in business have one, and if you don't, get one. A DVD camcorder will let you immediately see yourself on your computer after a presentation or meeting. Don't let today's technology gather dust. Use video to transform the way you see yourself and the way you communicate.

Previous generations could see their reflection in a mirror, but mirrors cannot be played back and studied. They cannot show you how the people in the last row of the theater see you. They cannot reflect your voice, so you can hear what you really sound like instead of how you *think* you sound.

Observed Behavior Changes

Video-cybernetics puts more self-transforming power in our hands than Maxwell Maltz ever dreamed of. When we see ourselves on video, we *become* the audience. We can see ourselves as others see us. And observed behavior changes.

Bonnie was a slender and personable lady of twenty-eight when I first met her. She was working as administrative assistant to my friend Patricia Fripp, the noted speaking coach and keynote speaker (www .fripp.com). Bonnie was effective and attractive, and Patricia spoke glowingly of Bonnie's skills. Unfortunately, Bonnie didn't see herself that way. Though she carried out her professional duties with apparent confidence, she seemed personally inhibited and insecure.

She went through our two-day workshop with extensive video feedback. Afterward, I asked Bonnie, "What have you learned?"

Her reply was succinct—and surprising: "I'm pretty."

That's all she said. And she *was* pretty—but until she saw herself on video in our workshop, she didn't think so. Videotape had shown her something that even her mirror couldn't reveal: She was pretty. Why was that such a surprising revelation to her?

I later learned that, during her childhood, Bonnie had been mercilessly teased by her older sisters for supposedly being skinny and unattractive. She grew up believing those cruel taunts were true—*until she experienced the power of video-cybernetics*. For the first time in her life, negative, false feedback was replaced by positive, accurate feedback.

Our behavior is profoundly affected by the way we view ourselves. A false self-image, based on all the negative feedback we've received over the years, distorts and hinders our behavior. Negative feedback sabotages our success and keeps us from achieving our dreams.

Most of the negative views we have of ourselves are hidden from our conscious awareness. It's not our conscious New Brain but our unconscious First Brain that says, *I'm unworthy, I'm incompetent, I'm unattractive*. These are irrational and untrue impressions of ourselves, deeply imbedded in the preconscious layers of the memory-laden First Brain.

Our self-image is primarily stored in the emotional First Brain, not the rational New Brain. The First Brain is visual and unbelievably powerful—so powerful that the New Brain is not strong enough by itself to reprogram what the First Brain is convinced it knows. You can tell yourself all day long, *I'm worthy, I'm competent, I'm attractive*—but that's New Brain information. Our primal, emotional First Brain doesn't process logic and words—but it does process images.

The First Brain must be convinced at the visual level. That's why a picture is worth a thousand words. For the First Brain, seeing really is believing. That's why a visual medium—video feedback—succeeds in reprogramming the First Brain when words and New Brain logic fail.

That's the power of video-cybernetics.

How We Learn

We all undergo a four-stage learning process. The concept, developed by renowned psychologist Abraham Maslow, is simple and profound.[1]

Stage 1: Unconscious Incompetence. We don't know that we don't know.

Two-year-olds are confident that they can do anything—but watch a two-year-old pour himself a glass of milk! Try to take the milk carton away from him and he has a fit! "Me do it!" he screams. If he gets his way, this little half-pint guy is going to create a half-gallon of disaster! Why? Because he's unconsciously incompetent. He doesn't know how much he doesn't know.

If you've never experienced the power of video feedback, you are in a comparable state of unconscious incompetence. You have some bad communicating habits that you're not even aware of—and what you don't know can hurt you. You need to become aware of your communication habits, both your strengths and your weaknesses.

Stage 2: Conscious Incompetence. We know that we don't know.

Now we're getting somewhere. Once you see yourself on video, you become aware of your communicating weaknesses. Perhaps you see some distracting habits in the way you use your hands or that tendency to use nonwords like *umm* and *uhh*. You wince—and you know you've got some bad habits. That's the bad news. The good news is that you now know what to work on in order to improve. You've also learned that you have some communicating strengths you didn't know you had.

Stage 3: Conscious Competence. We work at what we don't know.

In this stage, we make a conscious effort to master new skills and eliminate habits that hinder us. We practice, drill, and repeat the task. It doesn't come easily; nothing worthwhile ever does. But in time, we learn to communicate effectively as we consciously move up to the next level of competence.

Stage 4: Unconscious Competence. We don't have to think about knowing.

The previous stage was like learning how to ride a bicycle. We had to constantly think about a whole host of skills: pedaling, braking, steering, maintaining our balance. But once we learned how to ride a bike, once we truly mastered the skill, we no longer had to think about it. Riding a bike becomes effortless and unconscious. Now we don't think about how to ride a bike; we just do it.

Learning to communicate works the same way. While we are acquiring new skills and unlearning bad habits, we are conscious of every detail, and the entire process feels difficult and unnatural. But as we practice and master the skills, we become unconsciously competent. Speaking before an audience becomes effortless and unconscious. We don't think about how to do it; we just do it.

Natural Communicators

To be persuasive as communicators, we must be *natural* communicators. In every communicating situation, whether we are talking to an audience of one or one thousand, our goal is to be real, human, and natural. So we must become unconsciously competent in our communicating behavior. We need to be comfortable stepping away from the lectern, speaking from a few trigger words instead of reading a script, pausing instead of filling the silence with nonwords.

One of the best communicators I know is Jill E. Barad, who was CEO of Mattel until 2000. During seventeen years at Mattel, Jill became president of Mattel USA in 1990, then president and COO of

Mattel, Inc., in 1992, and CEO in 1997. She made her reputation by taking the languishing Barbie line of dolls and reestablishing it as America's most successful toy line. Her severance package at the time of her departure was a reported four hundred million dollars, and she is currently in great demand as a public speaker.

Jill went through the Decker training program around the time she became president of Mattel USA. She told me about her first presentation to the top executives and managers of the company after she became president. She recalled a moment in the middle of her presentation when she paused and looked out over the faces in the room. All eyes were on her. What would she say next?

"Honestly," she told me, "I didn't know what I was going to say. It wasn't because I was out of ideas, but because I had so many ideas. Should I tell a story? Use a quotation I had read that morning? The ideas were bouncing in my head like ping-pong balls—and it wasn't scary. It was exhilarating. Stimulating. At that moment I realized the power you have when you're speaking. I could go anywhere I wanted with my talk and the audience would follow along with me. They didn't know if I was sticking to my 'script' or not—and, of course, I didn't even have a script."

Within milliseconds, Jill decided to tell a story—and use a quote. Along the way, an absolutely inspired transition came to her that brought her back to her prepared conclusion. The applause was enthusiastic.

Jill Barad has learned the power of communicating naturally, of being spontaneous and confident while speaking before an audience.

Confidence comes as we build our competence through practice and repetition. The more experience you gain as a speaker, the more confidence you'll have in thinking on your feet as a speaker. When you are confident, trusting in the power of your amazing brain, you are open to new ideas and new situations. While you are speaking, you'll think of a pertinent story or funny aside that you can throw into your talk on the spur of the moment. You may get feedback from your audience that will inspire you to take your talk in a new and previously unplanned direction.

Put your mouth in gear—and your mind will follow. Trust.

Confidence = Mastery

Have you ever observed someone attempting a task for the very first time—a task over which they feel absolutely no sense of mastery? Remember your child's first awkward steps? Remember the time your dad put you on a bicycle and sent you wobbling down the sidewalk for your very first solo bike ride?

Mastery doesn't come from having someone hold your hand. Mastery doesn't come from training wheels. Mastery comes from *doing*, pure and simple. Nothing in the world can take the place of simply leaping out of the nest and flapping your wings like mad to stay aloft. As you *do*, you learn. As you *learn*, you gain mastery. As you gain *mastery*, your confidence increases. As you become more confident, you *do* more, *learn* more, gain *more mastery*—and life becomes an upward spiral of success.

Confidence is the capstone of all your communicating skills. People talk about speakers who have a "magnetic personality." Much of that magnetism comes from confidence. When you are confident, you attract trust like a magnet. Your confidence communicates powerfully and directly with the First Brain of your listener. When you trust yourself and your communicating skills, others will trust you as well.

In the Decker Communications training programs, we teach the skills that enable people to become confident, comfortable, natural communicators. The goal of communicating is to become authentic and persuasive. I don't want you to become a polished professional speaker. I want to reveal the natural communicator within you—your natural self.

The natural self has been inside you all along. The problem is that, somewhere along the line, the perfectly natural act of getting up in front of people and communicating with them has been turned into a chore, a struggle. So you bottle up the natural self that yearns to break free.

Build Confidence by Taking Risks

Building confidence to communicate is easy. All you have to do is risk. The trouble is that most of us don't like to take risks. We prefer the security of a sure thing. The problem is that sure things produce modest rewards. The greatest rewards always go with the highest risks. Safe is a dangerous place to be.

To get what you really want out of life, you have to put yourself on the line. When you take that risk, odds are you'll succeed. Success builds confidence, and confidence breeds more success. As Emerson said, "Do the thing you fear, and the death of fear is certain."

"I was scared to death," said Roger, a sales engineer. "I'm one of those people who's terrified of getting up in front of a group. I didn't want to be there, knowing I'd have to speak in front of people—and in front of a video camera. But I figured I had to take this opportunity for self-improvement. By the end of the seminar I was much more confident. The fear of speaking never completely goes away, but now I have a handle on how to channel that fear and make it work for me."

"I didn't have confidence going in," said Tricia, a marketing manager. "The confidence came after I learned what my habits were—how to strengthen the good ones, how to replace the bad ones. In everything I tried, I saw results. I saw change and growth in myself and others in the group. I walked in scared, but I walked out with a smile, feeling really confident for the first time in my life."

Tom, a teacher and administrator, said, "Going in I was fearful! But as I did my first couple of impromptu speeches and saw myself on video, it wasn't intimidating anymore. Coming out, I felt I had the tools and confidence not only to be a better speaker but a better leader. I do a lot of communicating in meetings, small groups, and team settings as well as in front of large groups, and the things I learned have made me more effective and confident in all those settings."

Nothing worthwhile was ever done inside a comfort zone. The rewards go to the risk-takers—and the talkers.

My goal in this book has been to challenge you; to affect you; to change your outlook on what communications is all about; to show you how to use the First Brain to *transform* your own personal communications. I know you can do it—because I've done it myself.

Many years ago I reached a nadir of my own. I had my own film company, and after some initial triumphs, our box office and contracts started drying up. I had to regroup and reconsider. I decided to set some goals and take some risks. Real risks. Personal risks.

One of the goals I set was to be able to get up anytime and speak with confidence. I certainly wasn't a confident communicator at the time, so it was almost too much to hope for. But that was my goal—and I reached that goal by risking.

I started speaking at every opportunity. I joined speaking clubs. I took speaking courses. I worked on my own behavior. For the first time I stopped hiding behind the camera and started getting out in front of people. I had always directed others; now I was learning to direct myself. And eureka! It worked!

In the process of trying to acquire the confidence to communicate, I discovered many of the principles in this book. By becoming a communicator, I was able to reach the other goals I set for myself. In a single year, I reached the level of income I had set for myself. At the same time, I also reached the personal goal of honoring a renewed commitment to my family—and I believe that the principles I learned as a public speaker helped to make me a more effective communicator with my wife and kids.

And do you know what *really* amazed me? None of these accomplishments required more work or took more time out of my life. All it really took to become more successful, to become a better communicator, to become a more involved family man was the commitment to *do* it—

And the willingness to *risk*.

I am not a natural-born public speaker. The speaking skills I have today are *learned* skills. I've made the transition from insecurity to confidence, from unskilled to expert. If I can do it, so can you. Here are eight steps that transformed my communicating ability. Follow these eight steps and within one year you'll be amazed at the changes in your personal impact—and in your life:

1. *Think First Brain!* Absorb the First-Brain concept. It is the lens through which you should look at all your communicating opportunities. It works. It's true. It will transform you.

2. *Know your strengths and weaknesses.* Watch yourself on video, then grade yourself in each of the skill areas. Acknowledge your strengths, then give special attention to improving the weak areas in your behavioral skill set.

3. *Focus on one skill at a time.* Don't try to make yourself over all at once. Be like the juggler, who starts learning with one ball. He then adds another and another until he can juggle four or five at once. Communicating is a juggling act of many skills; master each one in turn to gain mastery of all.

4. *Speak at every opportunity.* Make your own opportunities to speak at meetings, clubs, social engagements, and other events, both formal and informal. Determine your POV and state it boldly. Practice to gain confidence and mastery.

5. *Get feedback every chance you get.* Have a friend or colleague critique you. In fact, enter into a mutual agreement with a friend to practice these principles together, critique each other, and support each other as you learn and grow.

6. *See yourself on videotape as often as possible.* This is essential for objective feedback.

7. *Take risks.* Live the adventure of human growth, of reaching for the farthest limits of your potential.

8. *Just do it!*

Each time we ask more of ourselves than we think we are able to give—and then manage to give it—we grow.

Notes

Introduction

Page 4:

1. Michael Barone, Fred Barnes, Carl Cannon, James Pfiffner, "The Bush Presidency at Midterm: An Assessment," Heritage Lecture #789 (June 2, 2003), retrieved at www.heritage.org/Research/PoliticalPhilosophy/HL789 .cfm.

1. The New Communicators

Page 14:

1. Richard Zoglin, "I Was Trained to Ask Questions," *Time,* February 8, 1988, retrieved at www.time.com/time/magazine/article/0,9171,966611-2,00.html.

Page 21:

2. Oprah Winfrey, "How to Talk to a Crowd: Oprah's Advice to the Nervous," *O, The Oprah Magazine,* March 2003, retrieved at www.oprah .com/omagazine/200303/omag_200303_oprahspeak.jhtml.

Page 25:

3. Carmine Gallo, "Starbucks' Secret Ingredient," *BusinessWeek*, May 5, 2006, retrieved at www.businessweek.com/smallbiz/content/may2006/ sb20060505_893499.htm.

Page 26:

4. National Public Radio, January 11, 2005, NPR's Madeleine Brand interviews Ronald Fleury of *The New Jersey Law Journal,* profiling Homeland

Security nominee Michael Chertoff, audio retrieved at www.npr.org/
templates/story/story.php?storyId=4278721.

Page 33:
    5. Virginia Young, "Thanks to a Passionate Conservationist—Steve Ir-
win," media release, The Wilderness Society, September 5, 2006, retrieved
at http://www.wilderness.org.au/campaigns/wildcountry/irwin/.

Page 33:
    6. Brendan O'Malley, "Courage and Wit Won Fans," News.Com.Au, re-
trieved at www.news.com.au/couriermail/story/0,23739,20359806-3102,00
.html.

Page 33:
    7. Anderson Cooper *360 Degrees,* "Crocodile Hunter Remembered,"
aired September 4, 2006, retrieved at http://transcripts.cnn.com/
TRANSCRIPTS/0609/04/acd.01.html.

2. Emotion Versus Fact

Page 40:
    1. John Kennedy's quote and some of the source material on the debates
are from Theodore White, *The Making of the President 1960* (New York:
Atheneum Press, 1961), p. 294.

Page 40:
    2. This information on Nixon's attention to detail, and the quotes in the
following sidebar, "Dissecting the Nixon Debacle," are from Fawn M.
Brodie, *Richard Nixon: The Shaping of His Character* (New York: W. W.
Norton, 1981), pp. 421 and 427.

3. Your Personal Impact

Page 57:
    1. Author uncredited, "Profile: Brian Wolff," *Washington Life,* May 2005,
retrieved at http://www.washingtonlife.com/issues/2005-05/brian/.

Page 59:
    2. Todd S. Purdum, "The Clinton Legacy: Striking Strengths, Glaring
Shortcomings," *The New York Times,* December 24, 2000, retrieved at

http://www.nytimes.com/2000/12/24/politics/24CLIN.html?pagewanted=
all&ei=5070&en=ebfea69ea446fd4f&ex=1172293200.

Page 60:

3. Author uncredited, "Poll: Clinton's Approval Rating Up in Wake of Impeachment," CNN Allpolitics.com Storypage, December 20, 1998, retrieved at
http://www.cnn.com/ALLPOLITICS/stories/1998/12/20/impeachment.poll/.

Page 61:

4. Lory Hough and Aine Cryts, "The Power of Speech," *Kennedy School
Bulletin*, Autumn 2004, retrieved at http://www.ksg.harvard.edu/ksgpress/
bulletin/autumn2004/features/power_speech.htm.

Pages 64:

5. Maynard M. Gordon, *The Iacocca Management Technique* (NY: Dodd,
Mead & Co., 1985), pp. 76, 115, 134–135.

Page 64:

6. Bill Vlasic, "Chrysler Pitchman Proves He's Still Master of the Deal,"
Detroit News, August 5, 2005, retrieved at http://www.detnews.com/2005/
autosinsider/0508/05/A01-270715.htm.

4. The Gatekeeper

Page 72:

1. Detailed discussion of the brain causes some people to go brain-dead, so
I chose to put just the basic explanation of the First Brain in the text. Yet I
feel this concept is so important that it needs more detailed attention here.

After reading hundreds of books and papers on brain research, I concluded
that in the last twenty-five years there has been perhaps a tenfold increase in
the knowledge of the brain. And we *do* know a lot about the anatomy of the
brain. Yet it is evident we are still in our infancy in understanding the *behavior* of this phenomenal mechanism. No one has actually seen the neuronal
network operate as a person thinks. Nor has anyone seen the interweavings
of the immensely complex *parts* of the different brain system. We don't
know exactly how the brain works—we just know that it *does* work.

But we also have good guesses and improving theories. Brain researchers
agree that human beings have a basically "triune" brain, consisting of:

THE BRAIN WITHIN A BRAIN

Your First Brain is a kind of "brain within a brain." In fact, it is actually two brains within a brain. The components of your First Brain include:

- The brain stem—often called the "reptilian brain" because it looks and functions roughly like the entire brain of a reptile. Your brain stem is embedded deeply in the base and core of your brain. Its main purpose is keeping you alive—regulating your heart, lungs, and other vital organs as well as your sleep cycle. It contains the reticular activating system (RAS) that is responsible for alertness and consists of a network of cells designed for the rapid spread of excitation throughout the brain. The RAS is critical to the "fight-or-flight" response discussed in Chapter 8. It's the oldest and most primitive part of you, having developed more than half a billion years ago.
- The limbic system—often called the "old mammalian brain" because it is nonexistent in reptiles and was first seen in mammals between two hundred million and three hundred million years ago. This region in the center of the brain is the seat of human emotion. Drawing on studies of both animals and humans, researchers have succeeded in mapping specific control centers for emotions. They have even learned to stimulate pleasure, sexual desire, anger, aggression, elation, depression, and fear in animal subjects by surgically probing these centers. These emotions were originally part of the hardwired survival programs of reptilian and early mammalian brains. These survival programs, which are common to all mammals, including you and me, are hunger, thirst, danger ("fight or flight"), sex, and parental care.

Then comes the cerebrum—with its thin sheath of cerebral cortex, topping and surrounding the brain stem and limbic system. It is this thin layer of cerebral cortex—the New Brain—that has produced our civilization, science, technology, industry, art, music, literature, and economy—in short, everything from the propeller beanie to the space shuttle.

But it is the animal-like First Brain that produces our passions, that fuels our drives toward pleasure and survival, and that shapes our communication.

The brain stem and reticular activating system (reptilian brain)
The limbic system (mammalian brain)
The cerebral cortex

I have placed the first two parts, the most primitive ones, into a single category that I call the "First Brain." The reason is simple—they are complementary in dealing with emotion and reaction to emotion. Scientists and researchers generally agree that they both work similarly, and very powerfully, in directing our behavior at an unconscious level. They are also neglected by the general public and have traditionally been deemed unworthy of attention. That is changing. In the past, "Scientists were preoccupied with thinking, not emotion. Rational thought, after all, was the faculty deemed by the English philosopher Francis Bacon 'the last creature of God'" ("Where Emotions Came From," *U.S.News & World Report,* June 24, 1991). To join these emotion-related systems together brings their importance into focus.

The New Brain then is the cerebral cortex—the most sophisticated part of our brain, and it is conscious where the other two are not. It is also the most well known and emphasized, and yet it is only one part of our whole brain.

Today, scientists

are rejecting the notion of a human being as simply a "thinking machine," seeing human beings instead as biological organisms whose survival depends upon constant interaction with the environment. Emotions, far from being "trivial," contain, as one expert put it, "the wisdom of the ages"—warning us of danger, guiding us toward what is good and satisfying, signaling our intentions and our reactions to others. Emotions are the most familiar—and the most intimate—aspect of human experience, and they are gradually yielding their secrets.

It was only in the late 1950s that researchers were identifying specific brain regions that seemed to play a central role in emotion. But only in the last few years have high-tech brain scanners, new methods of staining cells, powerful computers, and other developments allowed scientists to begin systematically mapping the highways and traffic patterns of the emotional brain. ("Where Emotions Came From," *U.S. News & World Report,* June 24, 1991.)

HOW THE FIRST BRAIN PROCESSES INFORMATION

Your First Brain is loaded with an array of mechanisms that filter, modify, and channel incoming information. They work closely together, something like an unconscious team of the emotions. Although their intimate interweaving makes it difficult to see how each of them operates, scientists have thrown the bright light of research on the brain in recent years so we can begin to get an understanding of their separate functions.

The most basic mechanism is found in the core of the brain stem. It's called the reticular activating system (RAS), and it works something like a

"Flared like a wishbone, the limbic system wraps around the top of the brainstem. From its many structures arise memory, pleasure, pain and the brain's ability to balance the extremes of emotion."

Thalamus

Amygdala

Olfactory Bulbs

Hippocampus

Reticular
Activating
System

Brain Stem

"Gatekeeper to consciousness, spark of the mind, the reticular activating system connects with major nerves in the spinal column and brain. It sorts the 100 million impulses that assault the brain each second, deflecting the trivial, letting the vital through to alert the mind. "

From *THE BRAIN: Mystery of Matter and Mind* by Jack Fincher

telephone bell, signaling the New Brain that sensory input is on its way. When an unexpected sound or a flutter of motion suddenly attracts your attention, it's because this system in your brain stem has fired a signal (the nonverbal equivalent of "Hey!") to your New Brain. When you, as a speaker, use surprise, sound, motion, or energy to get and keep your listener's attention, you are ringing this bell in your listener's head. You are reaching the First Brain.

The main information-processing system within the First Brain is the limbic system, a collection of structures located deep in the center of the brain. The limbic system encompasses sensory input. One example: Have you ever had an immediate and strong emotional response when you first caught the smell of the forest floor, or of baking bread or cookies, or the salt spray of the ocean, or a particular perfume? Although your New Brain will later figure out *where* the feeling comes from (often housed deep within your memory), it was the olfactory bulbs of the limbic system that gave you that emotional reaction even before you became conscious of *why* you felt it. (Smell and the sound of music both appear to be another language of the First Brain, often triggering an immediate emotional response.) Scientists now believe that the limbic area it is not only the center of emotional stimulus, but it is the main switching station for all sensory input. It determines what sensory input is passed on to the New Brain for analysis and decision making and what input is filtered out and ignored. All the signals you give off when you speak (including your mannerisms, gestures, eye contact, inflection, and other nonverbal cues) pass through the limbic system for processing. If these nonverbal cues convince the listener's limbic system you are friendly, your message gets a clear channel to the decision-making processes in your listener's New Brain. But if those cues suggest that you are an uncomfortable or threatening presence, the limbic system will alter or block your message.

Part of the limbic system is a structure called the thalamus, a kind of exchange where most of the major nerve pathways of the brain meet and mingle. Here, messages destined for different processing centers of the New Brain are routed, shunted, or blocked altogether. Just as all roads once led to Rome, nearly all nerve pathways in the brain lead to the thalamus. In many ways, the thalamus is like a central switchboard that ties all the far-flung reaches of the brain together into a single network.

Recent research shows that the fingernail-size amygdala may play a greater role in our unconscious than previously thought. This almond-shaped organ of the limbic system, housed deep in the temporal lobe, communicates directly with the thalamus and cortex and works closely with the thalamus as a kind of "emotion central." New York University neuroscientist Joseph LeDoux found that the amygdala may make the first crude judgment of an event's emotional significance and then serve as a relay between the hippocampus and the cortex.

Another First-Brain mechanism that is critically important to the communications process is the hippocampus, a tiny nub within the limbic system that makes memory vivid. Some scientists have likened the hippocampus to the "record" button on a VCR. Your brain receives many hundreds of sensory impressions every second. Most of these impressions are fleeting and quickly forgotten. But during a time of joy, triumph, tragedy, or danger, the hippocampus detects our elevated emotions and (figuratively) presses the "record" button, causing all incoming impressions to be recorded in the long-term storage centers of the New Brain.

An article in *The New York Times* of September 24, 1991, announced research showing that the hippocampus also plays a role as a gatekeeper, linking various memory components in the cortex. This research also indicates that the amygdala works with the hippocampus in bringing emotion to memory. (Obviously brain research is moving fast, and we may not be certain of the exact links between thalamus, amygdala, and hippocampus, but we are certain that they all work in concert in the limbic system to control our memory and emotions.)

Because of the "record" function of the hippocampus, a highly emotional scene from a movie can stay with us for years; we can easily recall details from our wedding day, the birth of a child, or the death of a loved one. Even if we can't remember what we had for lunch last week, we can remember exactly where we were the day President Kennedy was shot or the day the space shuttle *Challenger* exploded.

Clearly, emotion is the key to making communication memorable. That's why, if you really want to get your message across and persuade people, you have to make emotional contact with the listener. You have to reach the First Brain. You have to press that "record" button inside your listener's preconscious mind.

Page 77:
2. Malcolm Gladwell, *Blink: The Power of Thinking Without Thinking* (New York: Little, Brown, 2005), pp. 23, 33–34.

Page 77:
   3. Ibid., pp. 12–13.

5. Getting to Trust

Page 89:
   1. Terry Paulson, "President Nido Qubein Brings WOW to Everything Done at High Point University," Leaderline blog, August 31, 2006, retrieved at http://terrypaulson.typepad.com/leaderline/2006/08/president_nido_.html.

6. The Eye Factor

Page 112:
   1. Professor Albert Mehrabian is probably one of the most important communication researchers working today. His study referenced here is often misinterpreted. It does *not* mean that verbal content is only 7 percent of a message, but that in an *inconsistent* message, verbal content will only be believed 7 percent of the time when compared with the vocal and visual signals. When there is no inconsistency—when a communicator is excited, enthused, and confident—there is no inconsistent message, and then this research is not applicable; the communicator and the message are one.

Page 117:
   2. Ron Willingham, *Integrity Selling* (New York: Main Street Books/ Doubleday, 1989), pp. 8–9.

8. First-Brain Fear

Page 171:
   1. This oft-quoted list of fears can be found in *The Book of Lists,* ed. David Wallechinsky et al. (New York: William Morrow, 1977), but the research was originally conducted and published by *The Sunday Times* of London, October 7, 1973.

Page 179:
   2. The several references to Dr. Peale here and in the last chapter are from an interview we had at his New York offices on April 11, 1991.

9. First Brain Under Control

Page 193:

1.The story of Major James Nesmeth is paraphrased from Zig Ziglar, *See You at the Top.* (Gretna, LA: Pelican Publishing Co., 1975), p. 85.

10. The Power of Persuasion

Page 204:

1. Steve Johnson, "Hypertext / Bill Gates, at CES, Serves Up Infomercial," *Chicago Tribune* Weblog, posted January 8, 2007, retrieved at http://featuresblogs.chicagotribune.com/technology_internetcritic/2007/01/bill_gates_at_c.html.

Page 205:

2. Duncan McLeod, "Apple Looks Peachy," *Financial Mail,* January 19, 2007, retrieved at http://free.financialmail.co.za/07/0119/technology/atech.htm.

13. Mastery

Page 245:

1. The Four Stages of Learning is now a common trainer's tool, but its origination has been attributed to the great psychologist Abraham Maslow.

Index